As an executive search professional who has placed CEOs for thirty-five years, I weed out wannabes from real leaders on a daily basis. Leadership is three things: creating a culture, creating a plan, and hiring a team to execute. Traversi articulates this and the finer points of leadership very well. This book is a must read for anyone who wants to fine tune his or her leadership skills.

> —Vito Bialla, CEO and founder of Bialla & Associates, Inc., executive search consultants in Sausalito, CA

This is a must-read for any executive interested in succeeding in the future. Traversi has clearly articulated a new paradigm of the leadership model. This how-to book is both instructional and provocative.

> —J. Michael Chu, founder and managing Partner of Catterton Partners in Greenwich, CT, a $2 billion private equity firm focused on investing in fast growing, middle-market consumer companies.

With the current state of affairs in world relations, politics, business, religion, and even the family, a new leadership paradigm is imperative. Traditional approaches to leadership just aren't moving the needle. The Source of Leadership is a powerful outline of a new model of leadership that leaders and aspiring leaders can ignore only at their peril. Compelling, enjoyable, and timely!

> —Carl W. Stratton, founder and president of Carlton Services, LLC

THE SOURCE
of
LEADERSHIP

EIGHT DRIVERS OF THE
HIGH-IMPACT LEADER

DAVID M.
TRAVERSI

NEW HARBINGER PUBLICATIONS, INC.

Publisher's Note

Distributed in Canada by Raincoast Books

Copyright © 2007 by David Traversi
New Harbinger Publications, Inc.
5674 Shattuck Avenue
Oakland, CA 94609
www.newharbinger.com

Quote from Martin Luther King Jr. reprinted by arrangement with The Heirs to the Estate of Martin Luther King Jr., c/o Writers House as agent for the proprietor, New York, NY. Copyright (c) 1968 The Estate of Martin Luther King Jr., copyright renewed 1996 Coretta Scott King.

Cover and text design by Amy Shoup
Acquired by Melissa Kirk
Edited by Jean Blomquist

Library of Congress Cataloging-in-Publication Data

Traversi, David M.
  The source of leadership : eight drivers of the high-impact leader / David M. Traversi.
    p. cm.
  ISBN-13: 978-1-57224-508-2
  ISBN-10: 1-57224-508-5
  1. Leadership. I. Title.
  HD57.7.T733 2007
  658.4'092--dc22
                              2007023352

09   08   07

10   9   8   7   6   5   4   3   2   1

First printing

This book is dedicated to my aunt and godmother, Joan Sheldon Conan, a leader who understood what is and all that could be, and who lives on in the hearts of many.

CONTENTS

FOREWORD

I first met David Traversi about eight years ago. On the one hand, our meeting was by chance. On the other hand, and looking back on it now, it was all by the design of some higher power. I think we have each grown immensely by having known the other.

Having sold millions of copies of *The E-Myth Revisited* and other books focused on empowering the entrepreneur and small business owner, my interest at the time was learning more about how small companies and their leaders make the transition to a larger scale. In particular, I wanted to explore growing my own coaching company and talking with leaders of large corporations about how to engage all of their constituents in the philosophies of *E-Myth*.

David, at the time, had spent most of his career financing and advising large corporations and their leaders, as well as running large corporations, and was looking to start businesses from scratch. He had an itch for learning what I knew and I had an itch for learning what he knew. Our conversations would go on for hours, and I think we each learned a great deal about the other and the other's world.

Several years into our relationship, David told me about his idea for this book you are now holding in your hands. I knew from our discussions he was a student of leadership, but I did not appreciate the depths to which his interest, and indeed, expertise reached. He explained his deep-seated belief that there was a core within leaders that fueled all the ways they were supposed to be, and all the functions they were supposed to perform, as leaders. He explained that this core consists of personal drivers, or energies, that, when developed, allow leaders to possess the traits and execute the functions normally expected of a leader. They "unlock" and "unblock" the leader. He felt these core drivers are the source of leadership. With them, leaders and prospective leaders would soar. Without them, they would flail.

I experienced two things following our discussion. First, I felt a renewed sense of connection and kinship with David. In my own work, I had recently begun to dig deeper into the self, seeking ways to unleash the personal energies deep within the entrepreneur. That work continues today, both in my workshops and in my books to be released in coming months and years.

Second, I began to notice how, indeed, the drivers David discussed seemed to underlie every successful leader I knew and had known. For instance, the leader who excelled at forming and articulating a vision for his or her organization was open, creative, and had a strong sense of intuition. And the leader who created a strong sense of accountability in his or her organization had a strong sense of personal responsibility and excelled at communicating in a highly connected way with his or her team. With every successful trait or function I could think of, one or more of the drivers identified by David seemed to be at its core.

With the publication of this book, and other books that focus on the profound personal powers that exist within each of us, I strongly believe we can expect an equally profound change for the better in our personal lives, our professional and social ventures, and, ultimately, our world.

—Michael Gerber
Chief Dreamer
In The Dreaming Room LLC

ACKNOWLEDGMENTS

As you'll see in this book, I am a strong believer in the oneness of our exis-tence, that we are all connected to each other and every other element in our existence by a single energy. Nothing occurs in isolation. There is no better example than the creation of this book. It would not have occurred but for the collective efforts and inspirations of many people.

Above all, I wish to thank my lovely and loving wife, Lisa, who embodies the energies discussed in this book more than anyone I have ever known. Coming into my life at a time of transition, she inspired and supported my search for a deeper truth, which ultimately led to the formulation of this book. I will always be grateful for the patience she showed, the sacrifices she made, and the space she allowed me as I put this together.

Thank you also to my sons, Carlo and Giovanni, and my daughter, Madigan, for their love and support and for the way they inspire in me the drivers presented in this book.

I have been fortunate to have worked with several mentors and counselors who helped me work through a number of issues that were preventing me from accessing some of the drivers, or energies, discussed in this book. In particular, I thank Larry Clarke and Beverly Engel for their patience, persistence, insights, and empathy. Without them, this book would not be.

I am grateful for Michael Gerber, my dear friend and former client. An inspirational writer, speaker, and generator of ideas, Michael encouraged me in the writing process and introduced me to people in the publishing industry who did the same.

My deepest thanks to my agent and friend, Stephen Hanselman, of *LevelFive*Media, LLC. This book was made possible by his confidence in me as a person, his ability to recognize the value in this book's message, and his broad and deep contacts in the publishing world. He is a class act all the way. And thank you to my outside publicists, Michael Levine, Liam Collopy, and Dawn Miller of Levine Communications Office, for stellar work in spreading the word about this book.

To my many clients over the past twenty years, my sincere thanks for their confidence in me and for sharing themselves with me. In my work with them over many years, I have been exposed to leadership in all its forms and qualities, and have gained a unique perspective that forms the foundation of this book. And a special thanks to the extraordinary leaders—coaches, teachers, and peers—I encountered early in my life who instilled in me a desire to seek a deeper understanding of leadership: Tom Whiting, Bill Silva, Mike Davis, Tony Kehl, Frank Martinez, Doug Johnson, Ples Crews, Marty Procaccio, Father Gary Lombardi, Casey Gilroy, the late John Ramatici, the late Steve Dunaway, John Volpi, Paul White, Shaun Bolin, Bill Vyenielo, Tim Burnett, Rey Serna, Dennis DiCamillo, Ed Conroy, Charles "C.C." Carter, and Scott Bootman.

Several close friends gave their valuable time to read the manuscript and offer suggestions for improvements. My sincere thanks to Marrianne McBride, who is also my sister—one of the most supportive anyone ever had; Stephen Gale, a wise man in the ways of both the soul and leadership; and Carl Stratton, whom I also thank for being the friend that he is and for his consistent support, insights, and enthusiasm over the many years of our friendship and various collaborations. I am thankful also for the unwavering support and grounding friendship of Paul and Linda Kruzic and their wonderful family as well as that of Lloyd and Evelyn Adams.

I deeply appreciate my brother, Stephen Traversi of Foothill Media, for creating the graphics in this book and the book's website (www .thesourceofleadership.com), as well as the logo and branding for *The*

Source of Leadership. And I thank Levi Ruiz of Fixed or Free Computer Services for keeping my IT systems up and running, always with a positive and supportive attitude. These guys are the best!

My special thanks also to John Ramatici, a lifelong friend and inspiration to me and multitudes of others. A truly extraordinary leader as a father, athlete, pilot, businessperson, and community member, he battled ALS with the same positive energy, dignity, and love and support for others that characterized every other day of his life. John, on behalf of the thousands of lives you touched, I say, "We will remember you."

I also want to mention some other people in my life who passed from this world during the course of my writing this book: my grandmother, Josephine Traversi, who taught me and everyone she touched the meaning of unconditional love. Gene Benedetti, Mary Ann Milne, Garrett Fogg, Misha Dynnikov, and Jonathan Field were extraordinary leaders in their own ways and arenas, and, like most extraordinary leaders, they inspired more deeply and broadly than they ever realized.

Finally, I was fortunate to work with a wonderful group of people at New Harbinger Publications—acquisitions, editorial, design/production, marketing, and everyone who helped bring my book into being and place it in the hands of readers. Thank you to the entire team for seeing the value in what I have to say and having the confidence that I could articulate it in an engaging manner. My special thanks to Melissa Kirk, my acquisitions editor, for managing the process with enthusiasm and class; to Heather Mitchener, my editorial director; Jess Beebe and Kayla Sussell, my senior editors; and Jean Blomquist, my copy editor, for their patience and commitment, and for ensuring I communicated my message in a compelling way; and to Julie Bennett, director of sales and marketing; Amy Shoup, art director; Earlita Chenault, my publicist; and Troy DuFrene, copywriter, for developing and executing a powerful marketing plan.

INTRODUCTION

I WENT SEARCHING

Do you have the desire to lead as effectively as you can? Are you willing to commit yourself to effective leadership? You may already be a leader seeking to lead more effectively. Or you may be an aspiring leader wanting to lead for the first time. Given the opportunities we all have to lead—in arenas such as family, business, politics, education, nonprofit organizations, athletics, or the military, to name a few—this book is for everyone. And, most importantly, it is for you.

This book addresses how to improve your effectiveness as a leader today—a time when we face the highest velocity, most complex, dynamic change in the history of our existence. It equips you with the best tools available to face these challenges—tools that will enable you to find deep contentment and fulfillment on a personal level as well as empower you to become a *high-impact leader*.

A high-impact leader possesses the classic character traits of a leader:

- Self-defined

- Forward thinking

- Credible

- Inspiring

- People oriented

- Energetic

- Curious

- Focused

- Courageous

- Organized

- Supportive

A high-impact leader also executes the classic leadership functions:

- Builds a values-based core

- Generates ideas

- Forms a vision

- Builds a plan

- Engages a team

- Builds a responsive structure

- Creates accountability

- Produces results

The tools you need to become a high-impact leader exist within you right now. They are *internal drivers*, or "personal energies," waiting to assist you in your journey. Accessing them is merely a matter of choice. Although the drivers themselves have been around at least since the beginning of the human race, they have generally not been discussed in the context of leadership. Thus, you will find little empirical evidence supporting the connections I draw between them and leadership. Rather, I believe, based on cognitions and perceptions formed over a lengthy career as a leader and an advisor to many of the top leaders in the United States, that these drivers comprise the core of the high-impact leader. They suggest an approach to leadership that differs greatly from any you have ever considered. They ask you to dig deep within yourself, down to your core as a human being, to tap energies that will fuel your ability to be a highly effective leader. All I ask is that you remain open and not resist, and try these ideas on for size. Just consider the possibility that the journey suggested here might be the most profound of your life.

THE GLOBAL LEADERSHIP CRISIS

Based on my observations and experience, I believe that many leaders today in a variety of arenas—government, politics, the military, social movements, religion, nonprofits, and the corporate world—are struggling and even failing. I believe, for instance, that our political leaders, as a whole, are doing little to reverse global warming and to ensure a safe and friendly environment for humans and other species in coming years. In fact, in November 2006, then–Secretary General of the United Nations Kofi Annan said global warming has been "caused by a frightening lack of leadership" across the globe (Gettleman 2006). Leaders do little to address the effect of harmful chemicals on our air, land, and water and to ensure that humans—and our plants, livestock, poultry, and fish—remain healthy. They do little to address our basic health-and-human-services needs and to ensure that millions of us are well-fed and healthy. And they do little to engender our confidence in their integrity or our belief that they act for reasons other than simply what will get them reelected. Internationally, they are ineffective in protecting us and ensuring a peaceful and safe existence for us and our children. Since World War II, have we ever felt more unsafe?

I believe that many of our religious leaders have disappointed us as well. You don't need to look further than the Catholic Church and its molestation scandals. And the corporate world? Many chief executives miss their earnings estimates because they are not able to grasp what is really going on all around them. Many err in product development and release a product that is either defective or incompatible with what the consumer wants. Many miss what is happening in the competitive landscape and learn too late that a competitor has trumped them. Many shrink in the face of this fast, complex, threatening existence and fail to take risks. They are closed to the truths underneath all the static and noise. Some, driven by fear, plunder their companies and shareholders. Others, in arrogance and greed, commit crime without compunction. We have all read about Enron, Tyco, WorldCom, Adelphia, and, more recently, the many scandals relating to the backdating of stock options.

Leaders got us here. And leaders are going to have to get us out of here. But right now, we are in a leadership crisis. We just don't have enough effective leaders. And we lack an effective way of developing and training the leaders we need. This book will demonstrate how personal drivers—core energies deep within a leader—are the solution to our global leadership crisis. In every crisis lies an opportunity, and this is no exception. I believe that those who are willing to immerse themselves in a new approach to leadership, one based on these core personal energies, will emerge as the most powerful leaders of tomorrow, leading in a more effective way than we have ever witnessed before.

THE LOCAL LEADERSHIP CRISIS

On a much closer and more familiar level, many leaders struggle mightily in their own day-to-day worlds. If, for example, you lead a business, you struggle with seemingly infinite, highly complex, rapidly changing issues in areas such as regulation, technology, the Internet, outsourcing and off-shoring, labor, workers' compensation, the "greening" of the workplace, product integrity, financial stability, and even natural catastrophes.

In the nonprofit arena, you struggle with changing trends in philanthropy, demand for services that dwarfs resources, difficulty in creating impact, and "competition" from the overwhelming number of other service providers. If you lead a government entity, you face the challenges of employee apathy, bureaucratic inefficiency, and the lack of incentives to motivate creativity.

In academia, you face declining funding, overcrowded classrooms, underdisciplined students, overly apathetic parents, or parents on a mission to lay blame. In athletics, you fight with diminishing integrity, performance-enhancing drugs, parental interference at the youth level, and criminal behavior at the adult level.

If you lead in social reform, you struggle to find a voice—a compelling message and an effective delivery channel—to unite people in the fight against discrimination on the bases of race, gender, age, sexual preference, and economic class.

Even at home, family leaders struggle with forces that contribute to divorce, domestic abuse, addictions, and academic underperformance of their children at best and loss of them into gangs and criminal behavior at worst.

As leaders in all areas, we collectively lack fundamental tools to address our challenges. But keep reading. *The Source of Leadership* provides those tools. We can and will lead better, be more effective, and create a better life for all.

OUR HIGH VELOCITY, HIGHLY COMPLEX EXISTENCE

Why do we face this leadership crisis—both globally and at home? Why is our leadership often mediocre instead of high-impact? In a word ... technology. Technology massively increases the amount of data we receive and the velocity at which we must process that data. As leaders, our response to the quantity and velocity of data is often mediocre. Our technology-driven existence overwhelms us.

In 1981, the year I graduated from college, no one I knew had a personal computer. In computer science classes, we wrote programs on keypunch machines, turned stacks of punched cards into a processing center, and awaited a twelve-hour turnaround. In 1981, FedEx first offered overnight delivery service. Facsimile technology existed but transmissions were so slow that no one I knew had a fax machine. No one I knew had a mobile phone. (An early adapter, I didn't have one until 1989.) What else in 1981? The Internet as we know it did not exist. We didn't have scanners. We didn't have personal digital assistants. We didn't have wireless. We didn't do videoconferences.

What did we do? We used typewriters. We used Dictaphones. We used landline phones. We mailed correspondence through the U.S. Postal Service. We took everything a lot slower, processed the data that trickled across our desks, and made sure we did everything right.

Fast-forward a quarter-century and all these technologies now overwhelm us with increasing amounts of exponentially complex data, downloaded at faster and faster rates. As a collective practice, leadership has simply fallen behind the pace of everything else in the world that has been accelerated and complicated by technology. Often we leaders are unable to distinguish useful from useless data. Even if we can, we don't have time to understand what to do with the useful before it quickly becomes useless. We're trying to "drink out of a fire hose." As a result, fear, stress, resistance, lapses in integrity, inability to focus, lack of personal responsibility, absence of creativity, and most importantly, a lack of positive results are the hallmarks of leadership today.

TRADITIONAL LEADERSHIP APPROACHES DISAPPOINT

Surely traditional leadership approaches have the answers, correct? Actually, yes and no. They do provide good, clear objectives for a leader, but they do not articulate the means of achieving them.

Traditional books on leadership clearly and accurately describe what a leader must be and do to be effective in the leadership role. I have read thousands of articles and scores of books, including the modern "bibles" of leadership such as *The Leadership Challenge* by James Kouzes and Barry Posner (2002), *Leadership Effectiveness Training* by Dr. Thomas Gordon (2001), *The Fifth Discipline* by Peter Senge (1990), *Built to Last* by James C. Collins and Jerry I. Porras (1994), *Good to Great* by Jim Collins (2001), *Servant Leadership* by Robert Greenleaf (1977), *The Leadership Engine* by Noel Tichy with Eli Cohen (1997), and virtually everything written by Peter Drucker, John Gardner, Max De Pree, Warren Bennis, Margaret Wheatley, John Maxwell, and Jack Welch, to name just a few. With few exceptions, they distill down into checklists of character traits and functions of what I call the high-impact leader, something like the following:

CHARACTER TRAITS

The high-impact leader is ...

- Self-defined: intimately knows his or her values, beliefs, higher purpose, and vision of the future, and expresses them clearly

- Forward thinking: envisions exciting, positive possibilities for the future

- Credible: possesses competency and displays consistency and congruency of word and behavior, such that others have a deep confidence in his or her abilities and character

- Inspiring: listens deeply to others to discover a common purpose, then gives life to his or her vision by communicating it so that team members see themselves in it

- People oriented: openhearted, with a genuine love for people

- Energetic: possesses a deep reservoir of positive energy and the ability to generate new energy throughout the vicissitudes of organizational life

- Curious: acutely inquisitive and eager to learn

- Focused: able to concentrate energy and attention in the pursuit of an objective

- Courageous: able to make the tough calls and perform the tough tasks; has a propensity for taking risks

- Organized: able to coordinate and direct activities in a functional, structured whole

- Supportive: strengthens others by fostering an environment that encourages the taking of risks, collaboration, self-leadership, and recognition; facilitates the transformation of challenges into personal growth

FUNCTIONS

The high-impact leader ...

- Builds a values-based core: creates an organization's ability to say, in the words of James Collins and Jerry Porras (1994, 54), "[T]his is who we are; this is what we stand for; this is what we are all about"; the organization's "stake in the ground"

- Generates ideas: a thought leader, identifying new associations and connections, and originating new or alternative concepts, approaches, processes, and objectives

- Forms a vision: processes ideas and possibilities into an organizational objective

- Builds a plan: creates and defines the optimal path connecting vision to results

- Engages a team: recruits, engages, and inspires people to realize the vision

- Builds a responsive structure: creates a structure consistent with the high-velocity, highly complex, interconnected existence in which we live; a permeable, flexible structure that is highly adaptive to changing conditions

- Creates accountability: fosters a culture and implements systems requiring each individual to contribute his or her share within a collaborative environment

- Produces results: achieves the vision in the most efficient, holistic, and measurable manner

THE "HOW TO" IS MISSING

Leaders and aspiring leaders know from these checklists of traits and functions what one must be and do to be a high-impact leader. But what they don't learn from these sources, I believe, is *how* to be what they must be and *how* to do what they must do to be a high-impact leader. They know the destination, but they don't have the means—the engine—to get them there. The "collective school of leadership," while providing helpful objectives and general guidance, has gone neither far nor deep enough. What we will explore in this book is the means—the "engine," or drivers—to get you to your leadership destination.

In the past, perhaps our life was slow enough and sufficiently straightforward that leaders could figure out the means on their own. Or perhaps high-impact leadership was unnecessary. Perhaps ordinary leadership—possessing only some of the traits of the high-impact leaders and performing only some of the functions of the high-impact leaders— was sufficient in those slower, simpler times: Times when they had three meetings each day, instead of ten and twenty. When they were expected to read four reports each day, instead of twenty and thirty. When they had five telephone calls each day, instead of thirty and forty. When they never received correspondence called e-mail, instead of receiving and trying to respond to two hundred of them each day. When they traveled on an airplane for a business meeting once or twice a month, instead of two or three times each week. When they had time to think about things, instead of being on their mobile phones virtually every waking moment when not with another person and, increasingly, even with other people. When they operated in a local, or even national, economy, instead of a global one. But ordinary leadership just doesn't work today.

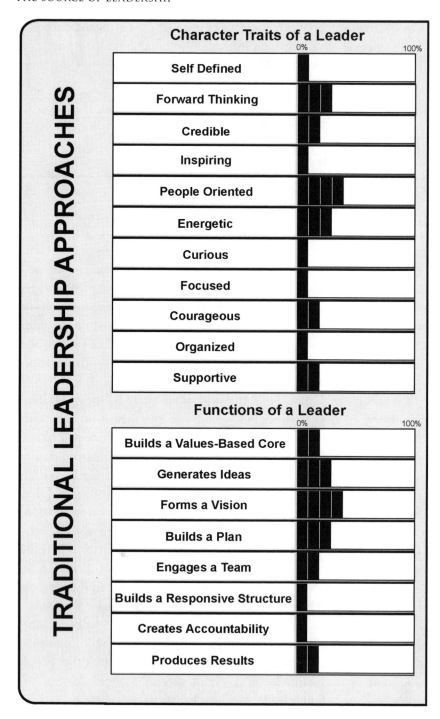

FIGURE Intro.1

Throughout this book, I use an illustration called the Leadership Dashboard to display my views of various aspects of leadership, such as leadership effectiveness, or the actual realization of traits embodied by and functions performed by leaders. The high-impact leader achieves close to 100 percent effectiveness in most or all traits and functions, while the ordinary leader achieves substantially less than 100 percent effectiveness in most or all areas. On average, I believe the Leadership Dashboard for leaders today looks something like figure Intro.1.

Some leaders may excel in possessing some traits or performing some functions, but in my experience, very few are "firing on all cylinders." On average, I believe leaders misfire on most cylinders and achieve effectiveness of less than 50 percent. In my opinion, very few high-impact leaders exist today. That reality significantly decreases the likelihood of our collectively going to extraordinary places and achieving extraordinary results. A radically new approach, a radically new way of thinking, and a radically new set of tools are needed to enable leaders to embody the traits and perform the functions of the extraordinarily effective leader—the high-impact leader—in this time of high velocity and complexity.

THE EROSION OF THE LEADER'S POSITIONAL ADVANTAGES

Technology operates in another, subtler but equally powerful way to undermine leader effectiveness. It causes an erosion of a leader's historical positional advantages. Until very recently, many leaders could achieve positive results over the short- and medium-term, despite their lack of personal preparedness, because of certain *positional advantages* over those they led. In particular, they had superior knowledge, mobility, and access to communication channels. They could choose how to lead based on their own perception of the conditions that actually existed, and they would rarely be questioned by those they led because those they led had inferior insight into those actual conditions. In other words, people followed leaders because they perceived them to be closer to reality, or that which actually exists.

Today, however, technology operates as a powerful equalizer. These positional advantages are gone. Those being led have equal knowledge via the Internet. They have equal mobility via the ability to work anywhere for any entity. And they have equal access to communication channels via e-mail, blogs, chat rooms, instant messaging, mobile phones, and podcasting. Today a leader must be closer to actual reality, or that which truly exists. Those who are closer to knowing what is real—what actually exists—will lead those who are more distant. For instance, in the past, only a company's chief executive might have had access to a well-substantiated research report suggesting an imminent decline in international demand for the company's products. But the chief executive may not have believed the report and thus chose to ignore it and led the company with an assumption that demand would remain strong for the foreseeable future. The company's employees would likely have perceived, based on the chief executive's actions and perhaps representations, that product demand was expected to be strong. Today, however, it is likely that the research report or its substance will be available to the general public, including the company's employees, via the Internet. The chief executive's positional advantage is gone. Today the chief executive must lead with the assumption that employees have the same information he or she has. In this case, to maintain credibility, the chief executive must either explain why he or she believes the research report is wrong, or lead as if the report is correct.

How does one navigate toward actual reality? By practicing, and ultimately mastering, personal leadership. Personal leadership involves identifying, accessing, and developing drivers—the personal energies deep within—that bring one closer to what is real. Let me share a little bit about how this happened in my own life.

DISCOVERING MY PERSONAL LEADERSHIP

Over my career, I have been, and in some cases remain, a corporate chief executive, executive coach, investment banker, lawyer, strategic advisor, and investor. I started out as a trial lawyer in Alaska and California, but quickly escaped into the business world. Armed with an MBA from U.C. Berkeley, I worked briefly as a commercial lender with Citicorp before joining Montgomery Securities in San Francisco in corporate finance.

Over the course of seven years there, I founded and directed the real estate corporate finance group, and also codirected the firm's financial services technology group. Leading initial public offerings, other financings, and mergers and acquisitions totaling nearly $3 billion for private and public companies across the United States, I worked closely with hundreds of America's top leaders.

After Montgomery, in the late 1990s and early 2000s, I held a number of executive leadership positions: senior vice president of E*Trade Group, the publicly traded online stock-trading company; president of Sirrom Capital Corporation, a large, publicly traded direct investor in hundreds of small businesses (since sold); and cofounder and CEO of PRE Solutions, one of the world's largest electronic processors of prepaid telecom products (since sold). In 2004, I cofounded Sensor Platforms, now a venture-backed, semiconductor manufacturer serving the sensor industry. Along the way, I served, and still serve, on a number of boards of directors of public, private, and nonprofit organizations. Today I provide executive coaching, strategic advisory, and leadership development services to executives and entrepreneurs across the nation. And I still start companies every now and then. Through these experiences, I have come to know and work with thousands more leaders in a wide range of industries.

For many years of my journey, wealth and professional recognition were abundant. But personal contentment and fulfillment were always "around the bend." I spent every bit of free time I had thinking about the future: "When I have this much wealth, I will do this." "When I have this job, I will do that." "When my kids are grown, I'll go there." Life was always going to be better in some way at some point in the future.

But early in my fifth decade, a divorce, a major career change, high blood pressure, and a fundamental realization that I was just not very happy spawned my own "dark night of the soul." I realized I had lived nearly all of my life entirely in the future. Through a slow, often painful process, I realized that contentment and fulfillment, and indeed the ability to function optimally in this world, are found neither in the future nor in the past, but only in the present. This discovery of presence, the first driver of the high-impact leader, and the practice of presence, opened my consciousness to other key transformational drivers.

I have had a lifelong passion for the art of leadership. Since my youth, I have been on a mission to identify the keys to effective leadership. I read every significant book about leadership written in the past twenty years, and built a huge file of articles on virtually every element of leadership. I went through countless leadership training and development programs. As described, I have had the good fortune of leading a number of organizations, as well as the unique opportunity to work closely with and to advise thousands of leaders in scores of industries.

My passion and mission were motivated by more than just curiosity and sport. I wanted to be the best leader I could be. I knew I was a good leader, but I thought I could be a much better one. But every time I read another checklist of the character traits and functions of an effective leader, I was frustrated. How do I better define myself? How do I generate great ideas? How do I engage a team in the most powerful way possible? I know what I am supposed to do, but how do I do it? How do I do it optimally?

I came to believe strongly that most of what had been written on the art of leadership did not really get to the heart of the matter. The best leadership books sold millions of copies and hundreds of thousands of people were exposed to leadership programs annually, and yet leadership as a practice never seemed to advance. The "how" of leadership development was missing.

Soon after beginning my personal search for a life in the present moment, a life that would hopefully include fulfillment and contentment, I realized that the self was the missing link in leadership development. By omitting virtually any consideration of it, the traditional leadership development programs make the huge assumption at the outset that we as leaders have mastered our own lives. That assumption is wrong. The overwhelming majority of leaders have not mastered themselves. And not coincidentally, the overwhelming majority of leaders are just ordinary leaders.

I began to observe and analyze the high-impact leaders and ordinary leaders with whom I worked as well as study those I'd worked with previously. I found that success and failure always boil down to personal characteristics. The more I studied, I found that success and failure as a leader depend on the same personal choices and practices—ways of being, deep within—that I was learning in my own very personal search. It was a dovetailing of profound impact! The drivers, the personal energies, that were radically transforming my personal life were also critical to being a high-impact leader.

As I studied each of the traditional character traits and functions of a leader, I found that each was enabled and empowered by at least one core driver, one personal energy, generally not talked about before in the context of leadership. Over time, eight core drivers emerged as dominant. Together they provide the fuel for highly effective, high-impact leadership.

A NEW DEFINITION OF LEADERSHIP

Over the course of several years, I refined a new definition of leadership that integrates the self and its energies with external results:

> Leadership *is the process of transforming deep personal energies—internal drivers—into extraordinary interpersonal results. The person who recognizes, accesses, and develops those drivers will first be wholly empowered and fulfilled on the personal level and then, and only then, profoundly effective as a leader of people in today's high velocity, highly complex, and interconnected world.*

I believe that leaders and prospective leaders who embrace this view of leadership and develop these personal drivers will experience a profound improvement in their leadership.

THE SOURCE OF LEADERSHIP: EIGHT PERSONAL DRIVERS

With this definition and understanding of leadership, we embark on a unique and deeply provocative journey that is quite different from those based on other works in the field. *The Source of Leadership* digs deep, far below the clichés of leadership, to reveal for the first time the eight internal drivers, or personal energies, that will allow you to become a highly effective leader—a high-impact leader—in the most exciting, albeit most challenging, time in history. It demonstrates how these drivers already exist within each of us, and how we can call these energies to our service. We can choose to access and develop the eight drivers necessary for the creation of personal power and then, and only then, can we achieve highly effective, high-impact leadership. We can choose to be leaders grounded in the eight personal energies. We can choose to be high-impact leaders.

The Source of Leadership makes the standards of highly effective leadership—described in book after book—achievable to those who follow its path. It will make all other leadership books more useful because it will provide you with the means—the "engine," or drivers—necessary for achieving those standards. It will change your very understanding of the concept of leadership.

Chapter 1 describes presence as the first driver of the high-impact leader. When you live in the present moment, you understand that everything is connected. Irrelevance is gone. Everything matters, not only in your personal life but in your leadership roles as well. You absorb every bit of life because you are highly focused. You think more clearly and efficiently. You act with more integrity and clarity. You are unburdened by unproductive thoughts of the past or future. You worry less. You fear less.

Presence is the primary driver of leadership, and provides the foundation for the other seven drivers. To use an automobile analogy, presence gets the engine started. It makes everything else you want to do with the car possible. It makes progress attainable. This chapter provides powerful tools for achieving presence, using presence as a solid foundation for the development of the other seven drivers of high-impact leadership, and for enjoying the many benefits of presence in your personal life as well as your life as a leader.

Chapter 2 describes openness as the second driver of the high-impact leader. Many, if not most of us, have learned through difficult life experiences to resist "what is." If we once felt pain in response to something, we close ourselves to situations that might involve the same pain. In some cases, this may be a form of self-preservation or protection. However, we often close ourselves off from opportunities because of unrelated pain experienced long ago. For example, if our peers teased us in high school for speaking up in class, thirty years later we might still avoid speaking in public. We are often crippled by fears and fixed beliefs that prevent us from seeing and experiencing things beyond our routine existence.

Fears and fixed beliefs are incongruent with a dynamic, rapidly changing world. Resistance to "what is" actually causes more pain and drains our energy. Opening to "what is" becomes liberating and energizing. We constantly seek to widen the net for possibilities, and resist nothing. This chapter provides potent tools for attaining openness and describes how openness directly enables a leader to be forward thinking and curious, and to generate ideas and form a vision.

Chapter 3 addresses clarity as the third driver of the high-impact leader—clarity in thoughts, emotions, and behavior. We have all, at least on occasion, thought, emoted, or acted out of anger, rage, envy, insecurity, guilt, greed, or some other fear-based stimulus. The sad fact is that too many people, and too many of us leaders, do it too much of the time. We work hard to maintain a healthy, clear *persona*—the appearance we present to the world—and suppress the unhealthy characteristics of our *shadow*—the personality and behavior energies that have been repressed from consciousness, usually since childhood. But we allow our shadow traits, such as rage and envy, to undermine our best intentions and drain us of energy.

When you choose clarity of thought, emotion, and behavior, you choose to honestly acknowledge your shadow traits and use the light of honesty and openness to manage them so they do not undermine your relationships, your pursuit of happiness, or, ultimately, your effectiveness as a leader. You choose to be energized. This chapter provides compelling tools and direction for achieving clarity, and describes how clarity in emotions, behavior, and relationships directly enables you to be self-defined and people oriented as well as to build a values-based core and engage a team.

In chapter 4, I discuss intention as the fourth driver of the high-impact leader. In every moment, each of us can choose intention or neglect, intention or disempowerment. While many of us constantly say or think "I hope" and "I want" and "I'd like," few of us sincerely believe we can bring about a desired result. Thus, we often cast our fate to the four winds or to the intentions of others. Last century, Napoleon Hill (1960) found—and documented in *Think and Grow Rich*, originally published in 1937—that the active practice of intention was the single-most important determinant of personal and professional success. Nevertheless, I have known very few leaders who practice this. Few have enough faith, it seems, in the power of intention. This chapter provides specific tools for employing intention to influence others' opinions and behaviors, and to change the course of events and conditions. You'll see how intention lies beneath a high-impact leader's ability to be truly focused and organized as well as to build a plan and produce results.

Personal responsibility is described in chapter 5 as the fifth driver of the high-impact leader. We live in an era where personal responsibility has been replaced by blame and litigation. These actions are fear-based denials of reality, and ultimately they poison interpersonal and work relationships. Personal responsibility is complete ownership of "what is," as distinguished from openness, which is the unbounded willingness to consider every element of "what is." This chapter provides compelling tools for owning "what is" on every front, and for creating the energy that results when we can say, "I am completely responsible for every positive and negative element that exists in my life." You'll see that personal responsibility is critical to a high-impact leader's ability to be credible and courageous as well as to build a plan and create accountability.

Chapter 6 defines intuition as the sixth driver of the high-impact leader. Each of us was gifted with a powerful source of inspiration—a knowing, an intuition—that is embedded in this omniscient energy that binds everything that is. But fear often causes us to abandon it too quickly in favor of a "safer" route supported by "facts" or the opinions of others. In doing this, we abdicate the crucial role that active intuition plays in life. This chapter demonstrates how to improve your intuitive skills, how to build confidence in them, and how to use them to build your personal and professional power. It describes how the skilled and liberal use of intuition directly enables a leader's ability to be self-defined and inspiring as well as to form a vision and build an organizational structure that is highly adaptive to rapidly changing conditions.

In chapter 7, creativity is explored as the seventh driver of the high-impact leader. It is the essential element of innovation, the commercialization of creativity, upon which the survival and ultimate success of organizations depend. Without it, organizations stagnate, decay, and die. But a creative, and ultimately innovative, organization depends upon a creative leader. Fortunately, every person has the potential to be a powerful creative force. This chapter demonstrates methods of tapping into that creativity and, in the process, of generating powerful energy. The chapter describes how creativity facilitates a leader's ability to be inspiring and energetic as well as to generate ideas and form a vision.

The eighth driver of the high-impact leader, connected communication, is presented in chapter 8. In the complex, adaptive system in which we live, where everyone is interconnected and relationships are paramount, communication is essential for survival. Once past mere survival, the better you communicate, the better your relationships will be. The better your relationships, the better your life will be. Better communication is a function of increasing the connection in your communication. "Connected communication" is far more than a leadership tool or mechanical practice. It is an intensely powerful energy—a driver—deep within the high-impact leader. On a connected path, the high-impact leader is present, mindful, and completely honest. He or she is clear and concise, acutely empathic, and in complete alignment with "what is." Everyone around the high-impact leader senses the integrity, the wholeness, of who he or she is and how he or she communicates; others gather strength in his or her presence. This chapter explains the system of connected communication, from clear expression of a purposeful message by an empathic speaker to an empathic listener, and provides tools for optimizing the process. The chapter explains how clear communication lies beneath the high-impact leader's ability to be inspiring and supportive as well as to engage a team and create accountability.

Chapter 9 puts it all together. It outlines a step-by-step program for using *The Source of Leadership* to embody the traits and perform the functions of a high-impact leader in our increasingly complex, dynamic world. You'll be provided with a clear map for identifying which traits and functions of the high-impact leader you need to develop, for identifying the personal drivers underlying those traits and functions, for enhancing those drivers, and finally, for becoming more effective as a leader as well as more fulfilled and content on a personal level than ever before.

As you develop the eight drivers of high-impact leadership, you will find yourself in a position of profound strength. With each choice, you will accumulate energy. You will find yourself clear of mind, calm, free of worry and regret. Your emotions and behavior will be stable and whole. You will be deeply intuitive, empowered by complete responsibility, highly creative, vested with the amazing power of intention, and connected as a virtual soul brother or sister with every other person in your life.

THE RESULT: HIGH-IMPACT LEADERSHIP

With presence as the foundational driver, each of the other internal drivers maximizes or optimizes one or more of the character traits and functions of the high-impact leader. One by one, chapter by chapter, you'll see a clear path unfold, leading you to empowerment and fulfillment on the personal level and then profound effectiveness as a leader of people in today's high velocity, highly complex, and interconnected world. Develop your internal drivers of presence, openness, clarity, intention, personal responsibility, intuition, creativity, and connected communication, and you will lead with more positive impact as well as find more personal contentment than you ever imagined possible.

CHAPTER 1

PRESENCE
The First Driver of the
High-Impact Leader

Concerning presence, the Zen master, monk, poet, and peace activist Thich Nhat Hanh (2001, 19–20) writes:

> Our true home is in the present moment. To live in the present moment is a miracle. The miracle is not to walk on water. The miracle is to walk on the green Earth in the present moment, to appreciate the peace and beauty that are available now. Peace is all around us—in the world and in nature—and within us—in our bodies and in our spirits. Once we learn to touch this peace, we will be healed and transformed. It is not a matter of faith. It is a matter of practice. We need only find ways to bring our body and mind back to the present moment so we can touch what is refreshing, healing and wondrous.

Yes, but how do we start living in the present? What does presence really mean? What changes will it bring? And how will presence make us better leaders?

HALF A LIFETIME IN FUTURE TIME

At age ten, I thought, "I can't wait until I am fourteen years old, because then I'll be an eighth grader and at the 'top of the ladder' in my elementary school. I'll get the special privileges reserved for eighth graders, like getting out of my last class fifteen minutes early to serve on traffic patrol."

At age fifteen, I thought, "I can't wait until I am sixteen years old, because then I'll have my driver's license. I'll have my independence. I'll be able to date girls. I'll be perceived as 'grown up.' I'll be a junior in high school. Everyone will look up to me. I'll be able to play varsity instead of junior varsity sports."

At seventeen, I thought, "I can't wait until I am eighteen, because then I'll be out of high school. I'll be an adult. No one will be able to tell me what to do. I will be completely independent."

At twenty, I thought, "I can't wait until I'm finally out of college. Then I'm going to law school. The work will be so much more relevant."

At twenty-four, I thought, "I can't wait until I'm out of law school. I am so tired of going to classes. I just want to earn some money and finally be able to buy nice things."

At twenty-six, I thought, "I can't wait until I get admitted to an MBA program. Yeah, I'm a lawyer, but why did I ever choose this profession? I hate it. Once I get through an MBA program, I'll have a lot of options. I'll start doing something that totally inspires and fulfills me."

At twenty-eight, I thought, "I can't wait until I get out of this MBA program because then I'll have a fulfilling job as a business executive. I'll earn lots of money and buy a new car and a house."

At thirty, I thought, "I can't wait until I become a partner at my investment bank. Then I'll be able to really relax and enjoy the fruits of all this hard work. Right now, I travel two hundred thousand miles per year, I only see my young sons on the weekends, and I don't get enough exercise. When I am a partner, I'll really begin to enjoy this work, over which I will have much greater control. I'll see my sons more. I'll exercise more and be in great shape."

At thirty-five, I thought, "I can't wait until I earn enough money to get off this treadmill. I am finally a partner, but so what? The work demands are the same. I'm still on the road constantly and see my family only a couple days per week. I'm not in the physical shape I should be. When I have $5 million in liquid assets in the bank, I'll retire from this and do something that really inspires and fulfills me. I'll be able to afford to be happy. I'll spend a lot more time with my kids. I'll do something about my relationship with my wife, which is pretty lousy and has been for years, for reasons I haven't had time to understand. I'll work out more and get in great shape."

At forty, I thought, "Well, I finally got out of investment banking a few years ago and began working on the 'operating side' of business. I am president of a company that is traded on the New York Stock Exchange. I'm in the process of selling it for an amount that will earn me almost enough to retire … or enough that I won't have to earn any more huge sums to retire. I can't wait until the sale closes because I've been commuting from the California Wine Country to my company's Nashville, Tennessee, headquarters every week and really want to spend time with my sons who are now eleven and nine. And I have to do something about my marriage. It's in miserable shape. One of these days, I'll get divorced and find the kind of relationship I have always dreamed of, and then I'm sure I'll finally be content."

THE PRESENT MOMENT

One day in my forty-first year, I thought, "My life is possibly half over. For every one of those nearly forty-one years, I yearned for a future day in which everything would be 'perfect.' A lot of the things I have are the things that I desired for years. I now have a good sum of money in the bank. I don't work for people anymore; people work for me. I have a pretty good professional reputation. I took on a new job as the founder and chief executive of a venture capital-backed transaction processing start-up in Atlanta, Georgia, and spend five days a week away from my family. Same old story. Have I made one real step toward contentment? No … absolutely not. I keep making steps toward something, but it certainly is not toward fulfillment, contentment, and true happiness. My kids are now twelve and ten, and I just haven't spent the time with them that each of us needs. My relationship with my wife is over. We just don't like each other anymore. Neither of us can even muster up enough affinity for the other to engage in any meaningful marriage counseling. I have been stubborn or stupid or both, but I have to admit that I am no closer to contentment than I ever was. Contentment must not exist in the future. It certainly does not exist in the past. Contentment must be in the present moment."

There began a journey that has changed my life dramatically and irreversibly. I began an intensive intellectual, emotional, and experiential study of presence and mindfulness.

In the past seven years, I have learned how to be present. By practicing presence, I came to profound new understandings. I came to understand, and really feel, everything as energy. I came to appreciate that this energy unites me with every other being and thing in one big undivided whole.

I will refer to energy throughout this book. Indeed, this book is about energy, or more specifically, eight energies, or drivers, that fuel the high-impact leader. What do I mean by "energy"? *Energy* is the capacity to produce an effect. The effect can be positive or negative, and it can vary in strength. Given that everything—every piece of matter, every physical condition, every unit of time, every bit of space, every thought, every emotion—has the capacity to produce an effect, everything is energy. As human beings, with the purpose of being wholly empowered and fulfilled, we must recognize, appreciate, and manage each element in our lives as a potential contributor or detractor to achieving that purpose. As leaders, with the job of producing a positive effect on our organizations, we must do the same.

With these new understandings, some of which required a lot of work and some of which just seemed to appear out of thin air as I became more present, everything in my life changed for the positive. I became more conscious of my acts and thoughts, and the effects thereof. I became aware of the energy flows in every situation. For example, I became more sensitive to the effect negative-thinking people were having on me. I became more sensitive to the effect positive-thinking people were having on me. I became more aware of my own thoughts and emotions and the effect they were having on me. I became more aware of my physical environment and the effect it was having on me. In short, I came to understand what positively affected my energy—boosted my capacity for having a positive effect—and what negatively affected my energy—reduced my capacity for having a positive effect.

I became aware of when I resisted ideas, people, and situations, and became much more open to everything in my life. It has been like being a child again, drinking from all that life has to offer. No moment has been boring since.

I finally confronted and resolved some deep personal issues that had interfered with my ability to maintain healthy, intimate relationships. I realized that I had significant anger embedded in me. Once I discharged this anger, I discovered and settled into a calmness, a clarity of thinking and behaving, unlike anything I had ever envisioned.

I learned how to direct my intentions—my specific desires for specific results—in a powerfully effective way. I learned how the practice of intention, described in chapter 4, ripens the seed of possibility into probability. I found positive things happening to me that some would call miracles, coincidence, or luck, but I understood as the universe responding to my intention and openness. I took more responsibility for everything in my life, stopped blaming others, and found that I was in more control of my life than ever before. I discovered a powerful tool inside me, intuition, which had long been ignored only because of fear. I allowed the seed of creativity, which exists within each and every person to the same degree, to bloom inside me. And I learned a powerful new way to communicate in a connected, empathic, and pure manner.

And I found that the driver of presence and the seven other personal drivers, which we will explore more deeply in the chapters to come, made me a better leader than I ever imagined I could be. The drivers, I discovered, play a key role as I—and we—seek to develop and embody the traits of and master the functions performed by a high-impact leader.

MOST PEOPLE ARE NOT PRESENT MOST OF THE TIME

We think a lot of thoughts every day. If you average a thought every five seconds of a sixteen-hour waking day, you are going to have nearly twelve thousand thoughts each day. Maybe you have more, maybe less, but you have a lot. I believe, based on what I hear people saying, that a large proportion of those thoughts for many people are negative, driven by fear-based emotions like worry, stress, and anger. Just listen and observe

25

for a day the amount of criticism, condemnation, pessimism, and gossip all around you.

While I am not a scientist, it seems intuitive that this negative thinking produces nothing positive. I suspect it is a major contributor to mental and emotional health issues that seem more pervasive by the day, such as depression, anxiety, stress, and addictions; physical problems, such as heart disease, high blood pressure, weakened immune systems, and obesity; and even negative social phenomena, such as high divorce rates, hate crimes, and discrimination. While I don't believe that positive thinking alone will cure these conditions, I do believe that negative thinking at best does not improve them and at worst exacerbates them.

So how does one stop these negative thoughts? By staying in the present. Negativity does not exist in the present moment. It only exists when thinking about a past event or condition or anticipating a future event or condition. In the present, there is no past or future. There is only now. Without a past or future, there is no negativity. For example, perhaps I worry that an employee I terminated is going to sue me and my company for wrongful termination. It has me thinking negative thoughts about this person and has me concerned about the time and resources it will take to defend ourselves if a suit is filed. Shifting to the present—appreciating the sunshine, if that's where I am sitting as I think, or the great qualities of another employee with whom I am interacting in the present moment—instantly removes me from the negativity.

WHAT DOES IT MEAN TO BE PRESENT?

We have all experienced being totally and completely present. Think back to those momentous times when you were overwhelmed by some event so that all thoughts left your mind. Your mind was filled with the experience of whatever event was occurring. You didn't even have room to think. All thoughts disappeared. You simply absorbed what was happening in that moment.

Maybe it was the moment your child was born. Maybe it was the moment your child took his or her first step. Maybe it was the moment your child first rode a bicycle without assistance. It might have been the moment you stood at the plate and watched a baseball coming at you at eighty miles per hour. It might have been sensing a kill opportunity in a volleyball game. It might have been striking a golf ball. Perhaps it was gazing into the Grand Canyon for the first time or standing at the base of Denali in Alaska and absorbing the view of a 17,000-foot vertical rise. Perhaps it was that sunset, the beauty of which defied description. It could have been your first kiss. It could be when you make love.

> *Presence* is complete awareness of the present moment. It is having no thoughts of the past or future. In fact, in its purest sense, it is having no thoughts at all. It simply means experiencing what exists in the here and now.

It may not have been a joyful moment. It might have been having a gun held to your head in a convenience store robbery, or watching a loved one die. Even in times of fear or pain, there is tremendous value in presence. In times of fear, presence helps protect us. In times of pain, presence helps us to realize the source of our pain and perhaps learn from it. I think we would all agree that in the deaths of our loved ones, for instance, the pain we experienced contributed to a much greater degree of appreciation for our loved ones still alive.

Presence is complete awareness of the present moment. It is having no thoughts of the past or future. In fact, in its purest sense, it is having no thoughts at all. It simply means experiencing what exists in the here and now.

The problem we have with being present is not that we cannot experience it. We have all experienced it at one time or another in our lives. The problem is that many of us are not experiencing it enough. And by not experiencing it enough, we are not living enough.

PRESENCE IS OUR NATURAL STATE

We were born to live in the present. Look closely at our children. They began living completely in the present. Their entire existence in their earliest years consists of absorbing the present. They see, hear, feel, touch, and taste everything they can. They are sponges. They are about one thing, and one thing only—experiencing the present.

What happens to them as they grow? Well, fortunately and unfortunately, they learn from us, their parents. They watch us every moment they can. They watch other people, too, but they really watch us, because, genetically and environmentally, they know we are the most important people in their lives.

The fortunate part is that we teach them how to survive in this world. We teach them how to eat, find shelter, communicate, earn money, and stay healthy. The unfortunate part is that, in addition to all the survival behaviors, we also teach them destructive behaviors. Most of the destructive behaviors are encapsulated within, or emanate from, the inability to be present. Our children see us worry. They learn to worry. They see our resentment. They learn to resent. They see our anger. They learn to rage. They see our shame. They learn to feel shame. They see our regret. They learn to regret.

So by the time we are only a few years old, many of us have begun to depart from the present, from the here and now, to places beyond—to the future and past. The slide from the present is a slippery, steep slope. Before we know it, and most of us never truly know it, we live almost entirely out of the present. The times we experience the present are truly notable, for their rarity if nothing else.

FILLING THE VOID WITH THE HERE AND NOW

Since life out of the present is nothing and since there is nothing in life but the present, at some point those of us who live mostly out of the present begin to notice a void deep within ourselves. We become inspired to find the reason for this void, this emptiness that always seems to prevent us from experiencing true contentment. Many more of us, however, and this is unfortunate, are not inspired to seek. We just assume our current state is the best that can be expected. We fatalistically accept that true joy is extremely rare, if even possible. We accept stress, fear, worry, anger, resentment, insecurity, and regret as part and parcel of life. We choose to merely survive—to stay alive instead of to live.

For those inspired to seek, to not accept the void and lack of contentment, I have come to conclude there is only one journey. It is a rich and paradoxical journey that is uniquely experienced by each person. Yet the route taken is the same for each of us. It is learning to be present, learning to live in the "here and now" instead of the "there and some other time." I once attended a seminar by Dr. Wayne Dyer, who refers to the present as the "now-here" and everything else as the "no-where." Same letters, quantum difference.

How do we make this seemingly monumental shift? How do we reverse a lifetime of living somewhere other than the only place life can be lived? How do we change a lifetime of habits as ingrained in us as eating? How do we change?

I and many others have found a meditation practice to be the best approach. In fact, for most people, being present is not possible without a meditation practice. I don't believe we can "intellectualize" ourselves into living a present life. I just don't believe the mind is that powerful. I believe we have to start living it, as opposed to thinking it, and meditation is the best way I have found of doing that. But I do believe that it is helpful to understand more completely our thoughts and emotions so that we can use them for useful purposes and in a more efficient manner.

THOUGHTS AND EMOTIONS AS FRIENDS OR FOES

You are not your thoughts. You are not your emotions, which are merely amplified thoughts that you feel in your body. You are not your mind. The mind and its thoughts and emotions are separate and distinct beings. They are products of your ego, not of your *true self*, which is the joyful, open, loving, giving, caring, nonfearing, and living-only-in-the-present-moment you that exists underneath all of the defenses, scars, and fears that have developed over time.

As separate beings, thoughts and emotions have powerful "survival instincts." The mind, in order to justify its existence, has a vested interest in convincing you that every thought and emotion has value and must be experienced. Your mind will use one of its most powerful tools, logic, to convince you of this. Your mind will tell you, for instance, that you need to worry about whether you will ever have enough money in the bank to retire, about whether you might go hungry someday and not be able to afford a home, about whether you might lose all of your money in the stock market. And it will create all kinds of logical arguments for why the thoughts are justified.

Our mind and its thoughts and emotions take us away from ourselves. That's okay, but we need to know whether we are leaving ourselves to venture with a friend or a foe. A friend will enhance our happiness, effectiveness, or chances for survival; a foe will do just the opposite. The mind and its thoughts and accompanying emotions can be either. Venturing out with the friend is fine, but there is nothing to be gained and much to be lost by venturing out with the foe. How do we distinguish friend from foe? Let's look at thoughts in the context of the point in time at which they are focused, that is, thoughts of the past, future, and present.

WHAT PURPOSE DO THOUGHTS OF THE PAST SERVE?

The past serves only one useful purpose: to teach us to live better in the present. Any thought that doesn't serve that purpose isn't necessary. In fact, it is harmful because it takes us away from the here and now. (Emotions, those amplified thoughts that we feel in our bodies, need to be treated differently and will be discussed in chapter 3.)

I find it useful to put thoughts of the past in one of three categories: loving, practical, or useless. The first two categories contain friends, and the third contains foes.

Loving thoughts make us feel good. When considering past loving thoughts, I immerse myself in them because I know I can learn something of value through them; I can learn something that will help me live better in the present. When I think of the joy I experienced as a sophomore in high school when my football team won the league championship, I try to identify the various things that combined to make it such a joyous time. I go back in time

> The past serves only one useful purpose: to teach us to live better in the present. Any thought that doesn't serve that purpose isn't necessary.

30

and feel the teamwork, the commitment to a goal, the hard work, the fellowship, and the love among my teammates. I then think about the areas in my present time life that could benefit by increased teamwork, stronger commitment, harder work, more fellowship, or more love.

When I think about how joyful I was when my sons were born, when I held them all night while their mother recovered from their deliveries by Caesarean section, I think about how my heart has closed to them in different ways since those moments. I reflect on how I react to their adolescent behaviors instead of embracing the sweet essence of who they are.

Practical thoughts teach us how to make better decisions in the present. When I reflect on mistakes I made in a presentation, it is with the intent of correcting them in future presentations. When I recall the route that I followed to my friend's house, it is to assist me in getting there the next time I visit him.

Useless thoughts are those that fall outside the other two categories. They should always be abandoned as soon as possible, in favor of the present moment. When I start thinking about how badly I handled a potential customer's objection and how we may lose a sale as a result, I may, at first, gain some practical benefit of learning from my mistakes. But when I keep thinking and rethinking this experience, my thoughts become useless—and detrimental. I'm simply beating myself up. To break away from useless thoughts, I need to focus on something in the present. It may be my breath. It may be an object. It may be a sound. It may be my love for someone. It can be anything that gets my mind off the useless thought.

PAST THOUGHTS CAN BE HEAVY

Marshall Goldsmith, the renowned executive coach, tells a wonderful story about how past thoughts should—and should not—be handled. It goes something like this (Goldsmith 2004, 103):

Two Buddhist monks encounter a distraught young woman at the edge of a rain-swollen stream. Dressed in a lovely bridal gown, she tearfully explains that she must get across to get to her wedding, but she doesn't want to ruin her beautiful dress. The monks look at each other, remembering their vow never to touch a woman. Suddenly one of the monks picks the woman up, carries her across the stream, and places her safe and dry on the other bank. In gratitude, she bows. He bows in return, then wades back across the stream to his companion.

"What ... why ... how could you do that?!" the other monk sputters. "You're never supposed to touch ... you know ..." While he scolds and lectures all the way back to the monastery, the first monk shuts out his tirade by enjoying the warm sun, singing birds, and beautiful flowers. Tired by their long walk, he retires early that night and is sound asleep when his companion shakes him and shouts, "You broke your vows. You should have let someone else help her. You are a terrible monk! You touched a woman."

The first monk forces his eyes open, yawns, and asks, "What woman?"

"The one you carried across the stream, of course!"

"That's funny," he smiles, "I left her back at the stream, but you carried her all the way home!"

WHAT PURPOSE DO THOUGHTS OF THE FUTURE SERVE?

Thoughts of the future likewise serve only one purpose: to make the future better than the present. Any thoughts that don't serve that purpose aren't necessary. They are harmful in that they take us away from the here and now.

When you catch yourself thinking about the future, quickly ask whether your thoughts are worry or plans. If they are worry, they are foes. Try to convert them to a plan. If the thoughts are about something you can control, formulate a plan to create a better future than you have in the present or a better future than you could expect without such a plan. If they are about something you cannot control, convert them to an intention or a prayer for a result. Once you articulate the intention or prayer, bring yourself back to the present.

If I find myself worrying, for example, about the prospect of my ability to fund one of my start-up ventures, I quickly sit down and outline an action plan and a schedule for executing it. If I find myself worrying about the loss of lives in Iraq, the prospect of a draft being reinstated, and my sons being drafted, I do the things I can do, such as write my congresswoman and senator, but before getting too stressed, I gently remind myself that the most powerful way I can exert influence over the situation is by formulating an intention or prayer and expressing it to the universe. With that accomplished, there is no reason remaining to spend any energy on the topic. Sometimes the return to the present can be difficult. At such times, I very consciously redirect my thoughts to present things. I focus on people and things around me and engage in something, anything, in the present.

WHAT PURPOSE DO THOUGHTS OF THE PRESENT SERVE?

My first guide in dealing with present thoughts is the following question: is it a practical thought, necessary to my survival or optimal functioning? If it is, then the thought is useful and a friend. Here are a few examples: Should I take the freeway or surface streets at this hour of the day? How should I respond to my board of directors' criticism of my hiring decisions? How should I organize my sales presentation?

If it is not a practical thought necessary to my survival or optimal functioning, then I turn to my second guide: is this thought based on love or fear? If it is based on love, then the thought is good and necessary to my survival and optimizing my life. If it is based on fear, then the thought is harmful and unnecessary. I need to redirect my thoughts to the present moment.

For instance, my thought as I pass a tattooed and pierced youngster in a crowded shopping mall of "That kid is ugly, he looks like a gang member, and he's probably very dangerous" is clearly fear based. It is a negative judgment based primarily on lack of faith. I need to let this thought go.

If I see a beautiful grove of trees and think, "Those must be sycamore trees—they are such solid trees with beautiful foliage," that thought is faith based. It is an appreciation of a gift of life.

Sometimes it is difficult, since we live in a world of grays and very few blacks and whites, to determine whether a thought is a friend or foe. If I see that same tattooed youngster hiding behind a tree in a dark parking lot at midnight, I might think, "I better use some caution and

33

steer clear of him. There have been a lot of muggings late at night in this part of town and he might want to harm me." In this case, it sounds like a fear-based thought or judgment, and it is, but it can also be characterized as a thought necessary to my survival or optimal functioning. It reflects my love for myself and my need to protect myself, rather than a mean-spirited judgment of a fellow human being. The result of this thought process is a necessary "discernment" rather than a judgment.

THE POWERFUL TOOL OF MEDITATION

As mentioned above, I believe that for the overwhelming majority of us, a meditation practice is necessary to start living in the present moment. *Meditation* is the act of calming and emptying the mind. It has been practiced by followers of Eastern religions and cultures for thousands of years. It has been practiced by Christian contemplatives for centuries and mastered in the last century by such notable figures as the Trappist monk Thomas Merton. The technique has existed under many names in many religious traditions. It consists of a variety of techniques focused on letting go of things that keep our minds busy and rob us of peace: things that cause stress within us, things like fears and worries about the future, desires for things we don't have, and memories that upset us and cause us problems today.

In meditation, I distance myself from what is not real. I know that the past and future are not real. Meditation puts me into the here and now. I know that my thoughts and emotions are not me, and therefore not real. Meditation takes me away from my thoughts and emotions. Meditation centers me, my true self, in the midst of universal energy, the energy—that is, the capacity to produce an effect—that exists within every piece of matter, every physical condition, every unit of time, every bit of space, every thought, every emotion. Some may refer to this energy as "God," others "Allah," others "life force," and others "higher power." It doesn't matter. When I meditate, I act harmoniously and in complete concert with the only reality there is—the present moment.

Many people have told me, "I don't need to meditate. I have my daily run that keeps me calm." I have been a long-distance runner since my early teens and I know that while running is a great stress reliever, it does not empty the mind. It helps to clarify thoughts, but it does not eliminate them. Others say, "I don't have much stress. I really don't need to meditate." Although stress reduction is a product of meditation, it is not the primary purpose. The primary purpose of meditation is to distance yourself from your thoughts and experience the present moment. The more you can experience the present moment, the more you will be conscious of the present moment and think and act with that consciousness. You will likely fear less, have fewer negative emotions, and have fewer negative personal experiences. You will likely love more, have more faith, and have more positive experiences.

MEDITATION IS BOOMING

Since meditation became widely known to Westerners in the early twentieth century, it has generally been treated as a "fringe," "crunchy," even "wacko" habit by the mainstream. More recently, though, it appears to be moving rapidly into the mainstream. I meet increasing numbers of otherwise traditional business executives who are exploring meditation as a way of preparing themselves to better handle the incredible challenges they face each day.

In 2003, *Business Week* reported a striking surge in meditation among the corporate set following studies at the National Institutes of Health, the University of Massachusetts, and the Mind/Body Medical Institute at Harvard University showing that meditation enhances the qualities companies need most from their knowledge workers: increased brainwave activity, enhanced intuition, better concentration, and the alleviation of the kinds of aches and pains that plague employees the most (Der Hovanesian 2003).

According to the same article, meditation has some high-profile corporate disciples, including bond-fund king William H. Gross of Pacific Investment Management Company (Newport Beach, CA), who often meditates with yoga before a day of trading at his nearly $400 billion money-management firm. Tech outfits like Apple Computer, Yahoo!, and Google are also signing up. So are old-line companies like McKinsey & Company and Deutsche Bank (Der Hovanesian 2003).

BENEFITS OF MEDITATION

The greatest benefits of meditation come after several weeks or months of consistent practice. I have had the best results meditating twice a day, but once a day also provides huge benefits. It will change your life immeasurably. Consistency in time and place is very important. You will find that you immerse into meditation much more easily when you are meditating at the same time and in the same place each day. If that isn't possible, however, just do it when and where you can.

The primary benefit of meditation is learning how to be present. Once present, or at least present most of the time, an entirely new kind of life will open up for you—a life of understanding, positivism, contentment, ease, high energy, integrity, fearlessness, and creativity.

The powerful physical and emotional benefits of meditation include:

- Reduction of blood pressure (Schneider, Alexander, and Wallace 1992; Simon, Oparil, and Kimball 1974; Wallace 1970)

- Reduction of cholesterol levels (Cooper and Aygen 1979)

- Slowing of the aging process (Orme-Johnson 1987; Wallace et al. 1982)

- Reduction of pain (Mills and Farrow 1981)

- Reduction of stress and anxiety (Wallace 1970; Wallace and Benson 1972)

- Increased intelligence (Cranson et al. 1991)

- Improved academic performance (Muehlman et al. 1988)

- Increased creativity (Travis 1979)

- Improved memory (Berrettini 1976)

- Increased job performance (Frew 1974)

- Improved job satisfaction (Frew 1974)

- Reduction of alcohol, drug, and cigarette addiction (Alexander, Robinson, and Rainforth 1994; Benson and Wallace 1970)

- Improved criminal rehabilitation (Bleick and Abrams 1987)

TYPES OF MEDITATION

There are many different meditation techniques and, arguably, none is better than the others, at least in an objective sense. The key is to find a technique that works for you. I was trained many years ago in Transcendental Meditation (TM) and it has worked very effectively for me. TM is a mantra-based technique originated by Maharishi Manesh Yogi in India in 1955. A mantra-based meditation involves repeating a phrase or word as a means of "anchoring" one's attention and activity in the present moment. It gained instant notoriety in the 1960s when members of the Beatles began practicing TM with the Maharishi.

I have also practiced breath-based meditations, one of which will be described in the exercise below, and find they are equally effective. The point of both breath- and mantra-based techniques is that they focus one's attention on something that requires no thought. They free the mind. They silence the mind. Whether it is a mantra or observation of the breath that gets you there is irrelevant. As a leader with a mind uncluttered by thoughts, and a body clear of emotion, your awareness and effectiveness will soar. Your ability to develop the other seven drivers of leadership will be greatly facilitated. You will be more open than you ever thought possible. You will increasingly experience thoughts and behavior undistorted by fear and scars from your past. You will begin to use the extraordinary power of intention to change events and conditions in your life. You will assume complete responsibility for the events and conditions in your life, which will further empower you. You will find yourself drawing upon your profound power of intuition to make the best decisions of your life. You will become more creative than you ever imagined. And you will find yourself communicating in a more connected and effective way than ever before. In turn, these seven drivers will directly fuel the traditional traits and functions present in the high-impact leader.

EXERCISE: A SIMPLE MEDITATION TECHNIQUE

There are many books, tapes, CDs, and websites that explain meditation techniques. Once you start practicing you will likely be drawn to a deeper study that will greatly enrich your experience on many levels. For beginners, though, I will outline a simple but powerful technique, possibly the only one you'll ever need.

STEP 1: SELECT A SPACE AND TIME

Choose a space that is quiet and free from interference. When I started meditating, I would stick a note on my bedroom door to inform my family that I was meditating and didn't want to be disturbed. Choose a time, at least initially, that gives you the greatest chance for a successful experience. For me, I have found that the very early morning, before I have eaten and while the world is still inactive and my mind is relatively relaxed, is best. The late afternoon or early evening, before an evening meal, is also a good time. The late-afternoon, early-evening experience is quite different because the mind is in an entirely different place after a day of activities, but the meditation is still extremely rewarding. Meditating too late in the evening is usually not a good idea because, while it tends to break down one's stress, it is also invigorating. The effect is not unlike what one experiences from a catnap. It will take awhile before your body is ready to sleep.

STEP 2: FIND THE BEST BODY POSITION

Sit on a chair or a meditation bench or cushion on the floor. Sit erect and try not to lean backward against the seat back; slumping backward against a rest tends to induce sleep. An erect posture with the chin slightly tucked is a hallmark of meditation. While it is difficult to maintain an erect posture initially, you will quickly "get in meditation shape" and find that it is quite comfortable and beneficial to your experience.

If you are in a chair, place your bare feet firmly on the floor. If on a meditation cushion or bench, cross your legs or tuck them under or beside you (toes pointing behind you), again keeping your spine erect. There are many different hand positions. Try different ones until you find one that works for you. I usually rest the back or side of my hands on my lower thigh in one of the classic positions, touching my forefingers to my thumbs. At other times, I open my hands, not touching forefingers to thumbs. I find that there are times when I am compelled to stay very much within myself (closed forefingers and thumbs), and other times when I am compelled to open myself to life (open forefingers and thumbs). Just follow what feels good. Finally, close your eyes.

STEP 3: FOCUS ON YOUR BREATH

Close your mouth and start to breathe through your nose. As you draw in your breath, fully experience it. Feel the coolness of the air as it passes through your nostrils and starts to fill your lungs. Feel your chest expand with oxygen. Feel its essence. Feel its essential nature—breath is our lifeblood. As you exhale, feel your chest contract. Feel the warmth of your breath as it passes through your nostrils. Continue this over and over throughout your meditation. You'll notice that every breath delivers a different experience, sometimes slightly so and sometimes dramatically so.

STEP 4: OBSERVE YOUR THOUGHTS AND THEN LET THEM GO

As thoughts enter your mind, don't resist them. Let them come and go. Just observe them at a distance, in a detached and objective way. Don't identify with them. They are not you. They are interesting things worthy of brief, easy observation, but not judgment or any additional thought. Then let the thought go and gently guide yourself back to focusing on your breath. Again, gentleness is key here. Thoughts are not bad and you are not bad for experiencing them. They are simply a diversion from what is real—what is here and now—and shouldn't be allowed any power over you. Thus, continue returning to your breath and you will find, almost magically, that your thoughts begin to lose their power.

STEP 5: EXPERIENCE THE SILENCE

Initially the periods between thoughts are brief. You'll experience a constant, gentle shifting from observation of thoughts back to focusing on breath. If that is all your meditation ever accomplishes, then it must be considered a huge success. And there is no way that a person cannot accomplish at least this much out of a meditation practice. In fact, you'll likely experience this in your first meditation.

There is a profound state, however, that you will likely achieve with practice. It is a place of such stillness, silence, and peace that it cannot be adequately described. It can only be experienced. You are completely awake and alert, but your body enjoys an extraordinarily deep restfulness and your thoughts are suspended. You are present in every sense. Mind, body, and spirit are grounded in the here and now.

The meditation experience is much different from sleep. It is better than sleep in at least two respects. First, your body rests much more efficiently when it is not guided by a sleeping mind that is dreaming and restless. Second, and more important, your mind is suspended from thought, and thus suspended in the present.

STEP 6: GENTLY EMERGE

When twenty minutes have passed, take the next couple of minutes to gently emerge. Open your eyes, look around, start to move your body, and make a mental note of the way you feel. Early in your meditation practice, you'll be checking your watch several times, and that is okay. As you progress, you'll develop a keen sense of when twenty minutes have passed.

EXERCISE:
FOCUS YOUR ATTENTION

Although meditation is by far the best method for shifting into the present moment and achieving maximum mindfulness, there are other things you can do to shift toward presence. For instance, be acutely aware of your surroundings. If I find my mind too jumbled with thoughts during the day, and meditation isn't convenient, I focus exclusively on what I am doing and my immediate surroundings. If I am walking down a street, I may focus on the sidewalk, giving my complete attention to the place where I will next step. I may focus on the feeling of my feet hitting the ground with each step. I may watch each car that passes, absorbing as much detail as I can in the few seconds it takes for it to approach and pass me. If I am sitting somewhere, I close my eyes and listen closely to each sound around me. I just seek a singular focus. As thoughts enter my mind, I gently shift back to my singular focus. The more you do this, the better you get and the less thoughts are able to control your mind.

EXERCISE:
JOURNAL GRATITUDE

Buy a blank journal and set aside times to write down everything for which you are grateful. Expressions of gratitude can only be made in a present state. Go on for as long as you feel comfortable. This is an amazingly powerful exercise. In addition to grounding you in present time, it will rid you of worry, stress, depression, or sadness.

PRESENCE OPENS A NEW WORLD OF INSIGHT AND UNDERSTANDING

Once you begin living in the present, and you have removed the distractions of the past and future, you will open to the world and life in a way you never have before. Your life will change, and only for the positive.

You will understand, in fact you will feel, truths that will transform your personal life and your professional life as a leader.

Many of the epiphanies I experienced as I became more present revolved around the basic conditions of our existence, or what is known as "new science." As a schoolboy, I was educated in "old science," or the beliefs of Isaac Newton and René Descartes that prevailed from the late seventeenth century to the early twentieth century. Those beliefs held that an understanding of the whole of existence can be achieved by studying the parts. They held that events happen because something causes them to happen. For everything, there is a cause and an effect. Each cause and effect is identifiable. And everything happens according to fixed physical laws. They held that the universe is orderly, predictable, following natural laws, and works like a complicated yet well-oiled machine.

In the twentieth century, though, scientific thought was turned upside down. Scientists like Max Planck, Albert Einstein, Werner Heisenberg, Niels Bohr, John Bell, and David Bohm studied existence at the nuclear level and suggested that the causal laws of physics do not hold true. They suggested that cause and effect are not mechanical and predictable, and that physical laws do not orchestrate our existence. Throughout the twentieth century and continuing today, the work of the great physicists has been about studying the whole. It has been based on the hypothesis that every element in this existence is part of a greater whole and that, as parts of this greater whole, these elements are related and connected. No element exists independent of another. The work of physicists today, the "new science," revolves around how this oneness operates. Some key principles of new science are described by Joseph Jaworski (1996) in *Synchronicity*, Gary Zukav (1979) in *The Dancing Wu Li Masters*, and Margaret Wheatley (1999) in *Leadership and the New Science*. Let's look at some of those principles now.

EVERYTHING IS ENERGY

As discussed earlier in this chapter, energy is the capacity to produce an effect. The effect can be positive or negative, and it can vary in strength. Given that everything—every piece of matter, every physical condition, every unit of time, every bit of space, every thought, every emotion, every word, every vision, every color, every sound—has the capacity to produce an effect, everything is energy. We know Einstein and his progeny proved all of this in the twentieth century, yet most of us have probably not fully appreciated its significance for ourselves or the world around us. It's even less likely that we have found ways to concretely incorporate this knowledge in our daily lives. What might "everything is energy" mean for you in your life?

When you understand yourself as an *energy body*—that is, as an intricate energy system—existing in an infinite field of other energy systems, you will likely find that you cannot live life as you did before. The rules are different. The rewards are different. The consequences are different.

Let's look, for example, at the effect of anger on other people. Anger is energy, and as energy, it impacts the energy of those to whom it is directed. If you, as a leader, are prone to anger on occasion, you can no longer assume that your anger has no negative consequences. You can't just say you're sorry, or assume that the passage of time will heal whatever damage you did. You have to be mindful that your anger had an irrevocable, and very likely negative, effect. Likewise, acts of charity, kindness, and love have a permanent and positive energetic effect, even if no one is aware of them. As a leader, you transform your own personal energies or internal drivers (the eight discussed in this book) as well as other energies within your reach—ideas, people, capital, hard assets, intangible assets—into organizational results. For instance, you transform your clarity of thought and behavior into the ability to be self-defined and people oriented, and to build a values-based core in your organization and engage your team in the pursuit of the organizational objectives. And you transform your openness into the ability to be intensely curious and forward thinking, and generate ideas and form a vision for your organization.

THIS ENERGY CONNECTS EVERYTHING AND EVERYONE IN ONE WHOLE

You can think of energy as a vibration that exists within everything, every person, and every tangible and intangible thing, thus linking all things and persons in one whole system. We are inextricably connected with each other and everything in our existence. Nothing is separate and nothing is independent.

Joseph Jaworski (1996, 80–81), an expert on modern leadership, describes a fascinating conversation he had with the famous physicist Dr. David Bohm in London in 1980. Describing the implications of wholeness and oneness, Bohm said:

> Yourself is actually the whole of mankind. That's the idea of implicate order—that everything is enfolded in everything. The entire past is enfolded into each one of us in a very subtle way. If you reach deeply into yourself, you are reaching into the very essence of mankind. When you do this, you will be led into the generating depth of consciousness that is common to the whole of mankind and that has the whole of mankind enfolded in it. The individual's ability to be sensitive to that becomes the key to the change of mankind. We are all connected. If this could be taught, and if people could understand it, we would have a different consciousness.
>
> At present, people create barriers between each other by their fragmentary thought. Each one operates separately. When these barriers have dissolved, then there arises one mind, where they are all one unit, but each person also retains his or her own individual awareness. That one mind will still exist even when they separate, and when they come together it will be as if they hadn't separated. It's actually a single intelligence that works with people who are moving in relationship with one another. Cues that pass from one to the other are being picked up with the same awareness, just as we pick up cues in riding bicycles or skiing. Therefore, these people are really all one. The separation between them is not blocking. They are all pulling together.

In essence, we live in a *complex adaptive system*. It is *complex* in that everything is joined together in an inseparable whole. It is *adaptive* in that everything, as it strives to survive and thrive, dynamically adjusts to its constantly changing environment. And this occurs in a *system* that is interconnected and interdependent.

Even before new science, humankind has known this truth. Each of the major faiths, including Christianity, Islam, Buddhism, and Hinduism, is based on the assumption of an interconnected, interdependent world. Whether one subscribes to one particular religion or another, or no religion, is irrelevant. I can optimize my experience in life while believing the specific doctrines of any of these religions or none of them. But I cannot optimize my experience without understanding the principle of oneness and truly believing in my heart that we are all part of the same whole and that we are connected with every other person, animal, plant, and element that exists.

True appreciation of oneness was, for me, life altering. Appreciating that everything—every thought, condition, event, observation, and action—is connected in one whole took on a significance and meaning I had never considered before. Everything seems relevant. Everything seems possible. As a leader, I came to feel a sense of profound empowerment. I came to believe that I could have whatever impact I desired because the connections already existed between me and success, and my only task was to identify and manage them. Once you experience this cognition, I believe you cannot help but be a better person, live a better life, and become a better leader. You will be more productive and content. In the aggregate, people understanding this reality will make choices that enhance instead of destroy life.

Dr. David Hawkins, one of the great students and teachers of energy, writes:

> In this interconnected universe, every improvement we make in our private world improves the world at large for everyone. We all float on the collective level of consciousness of mankind so that any increment we add comes back to us. We all add to our common buoyancy by our efforts to benefit life. What we do to serve life automatically benefits all of us because we're all included in that which is life. We *are* life. It is a scientific fact that "what is good for you is good for me." (Hawkins 1995, 128)

As a leader, you understand that nothing in your environment is irrelevant. Any element in your environment may have the potential of significantly affecting your ability to lead. Every element is connected to every other element, and the more connections, and more valuable connections, you can identify, the more value you will create through your leadership.

ENERGY CAN NEITHER BE CREATED NOR DESTROYED

Energy can only be transformed from one form to another. Since thoughts and acts are energy, every thought and act transforms energy into something positive or negative. The power of this is astounding. Let's say you actually think a thought every five seconds, or twelve thousand thoughts each day, and the majority, or even a large minority, are negative. Since most acts are products of thoughts, it is reasonable to assume that a majority, or large minority, of acts are negative as well. Just think about how each of our worlds, and our collective world, would change for the better if those ratios were reversed in favor of positive thoughts and acts.

As a leader, you are highly sensitive to the power of every one of your thoughts and actions. Given that you affect the lives of many people, you are careful to use this transformative power in the most positive, value-producing manner possible.

WHAT IS OBSERVED IS AFFECTED BY THE ACT OF OBSERVATION

When we observe something, that act of observation changes what we observe. Spectator sports are a great example. Every athlete will tell you the crowd is an energy, and that energy has a significant impact on his or her performance. As a leader, when we watch one of our senior managers do her job, that act of observing has an effect on her performance—hopefully a positive effect, but an effect neverthe-less. Given that everything is energy, this shouldn't come as a surprise. Again, the implications of this are profound. Every time we focus on something, our expectations, intentions, hopes, fears, doubts, envy, and every other thought and emotion operate to affect that on which we are focused. When we have completely internalized the concept that what is observed is affected by the act of observing, when we completely believe it, there is no way we can ever observe anything unconsciously again. We will know that we are partially responsible for whatever we observe. We will know that we can change what we observe.

As a leader, given that your attention has the power to transform people, events, conditions, and results, this principle imposes a tremendous responsibility upon you.

FOR EVERY ACTION, THERE IS AN EQUAL AND OPPOSITE REACTION

This is actually a holdover from old science. It is Isaac Newton's third law of motion. It is one of Newton's rules that survived new science scrutiny. Essentially, it says you receive from the world what you give to it—what today is sometimes called "karma." Every action that has not yet resulted in the reaction is just the first part of a process that has not yet been completed. It is an energy imbalance that awaits balancing. The balancing event may not occur near, in time or space, the first event. In fact, some belief systems hold that it may even occur in another lifetime. But it will occur. It is a law of nature.

For instance, if you terminate an employee purely out of spite, for no reason other than you just don't like his or her personality, and then fabricate a legally defensible reason such as inadequate performance, you have done something wrong and, in effect, the world will retaliate. You have intentionally directed negative energy to someone, in the form of a wrongful termination, and you must await the moment, which may not occur for many years, when you are treated wrongfully by someone, often with no relation to the person you mistreated. Conversely, if you make a large personal contribution of time or money to a charitable cause, whether it is publicized or not, you can be pleased to know that, at some point, you will receive a positive effect equal to the effect you had on the charitable cause. Perhaps the effect will be personal satisfaction and will be immediate. Or maybe it will be a donation from someone in the future to a new cause you care about. Personally, although Isaac Newton talks about an "equal" and opposite reaction, I like to think that reactions are a great multiple of the action: Do something good, and it comes back to me ten times over. Do something bad, and it comes back to me ten times over.

As a leader, you are highly sensitive to the fact that no one, including you, is given a pass on this law. With the organization you lead, you have the power to create large effects. You exercise that power knowing that large effects will come back to you and your team, and you want them to be positive.

GREAT SENSITIVITY TO SMALL CHANGES

Complex and unpredictable results will occur in systems that are sensitive to small changes. Known as the "butterfly effect," this principle holds, for example, that the flapping of a butterfly's wings in Brazil could cause tiny atmospheric changes which, over a period of time, could cause a tornado in Texas (Wheatley 1999). There is no such thing as insignificance. Every movement of energy has significance.

Again, once we truly comprehend this, can we ever be unconscious again? Can we ever toss even the tiniest gum wrapper out a car window? Can we ever say something mean or condescending to someone? Can we ever drive a car in a hurried, negligent rush again? Understanding that the complex and unpredictable results can be positive or negative, depending upon the nature of the cause, won't we be inspired to think faith- and love-based thoughts and act with faith and love?

As a leader, you realize that the smallest thoughts you have and actions you take, as well as those of your team, have the potential of creating huge effects. You assume the burden of that responsibility and the enormity of the opportunity.

ORDER ALWAYS EMERGES FROM CHAOS, ALBEIT UNPREDICTABLY

New science has found that, out of our apparently chaotic existence, an order always emerges (Wheatley 1999). Unfortunately, at least at the current time, the type of order cannot be predicted. We just know that some order will result. Scientists have used computers to model almost every random behavior you can imagine—weather patterns, stock market results, epidemics—and the results are extraordinary. Definite patterns, reflecting an inherent order, are very clear.

As a leader who knows that order will result from apparent chaos, you trust more. You allow situations and organizations more time to run, often in apparent chaos, because you know that an order will emerge. You structure less and liberate more. You micromanage less and empower more. You direct less and provoke more.

WE STILL LIVE UNDER OLD SCIENCE ... AT GREAT RISK

Despite the fact that new science began to evolve a century ago, the principles have had little impact on our perception of ourselves, our society, or the world around us. For the past several hundred years, and still today, most people adhere to the mechanistic Newtonian view. They still believe that science and the scientific method can fully understand physical reality and use that understanding to predict and guide the future. This belief remains incorporated in our social institutions. Most schools, businesses, political structures, and organizations still operate as if the universe is predictable; still believe that ambiguity is a reflection of lack of good information or lack of a good theory; that there are absolutes; that answers are binary; that universal existence is hierarchical; that human-made systems must be hierarchical as well; that the universe is composed of isolated, separate physical parts; and that we somehow exist outside the physical world and everything in the physical world is to be conquered and used. Look around. Look deep. You will see that we are living as if old science still ruled the day.

We live under the guidance of old science, however, at our great risk. When our beliefs, practices, institutions, structures, and organizations are diametrically opposed to the laws of nature, something is bound to go awry. Ultimately, something will give way. Something will break.

The most insightful people, those present people who understand the nature of life, will flourish and prosper because they see our existence for what it is. They will not be in conflict with nature. They understand energy, and how to use it. They understand oneness and the interconnectedness of everything. They understand cause and effect, not in the precise manner of old science, but in the more general, more powerful way that compels us to be conscious of all thoughts and acts. They understand and appreciate the chaotic nature of our existence, and trust in the emergence of order.

49

The High-Impact Leader Empowered by Presence—and the Ordinary, Unempowered Leader

There is no better example of the benefits to American leaders of being present and understanding new science, and the serious consequences of not being present and ignoring it, than the economic boom now occurring in China. As this is written, many American manufacturers are being bankrupted as a result of competition by Chinese manufacturers or American companies who have embraced Chinese manufacturing opportunities. Conversely, those Chinese manufacturers and American companies doing business in China are enjoying huge success.

Why are some failing and others flourishing? It is simple: the ordinary leader with a furniture manufacturing business that had thrived through the booming 1990s thought of China as separate from himself. He feared the language and cultural barriers. He worried about the political situation in China. He believed that the Chinese couldn't produce goods of sufficient quality. He feared. He distrusted. He distanced himself. He failed to recognize that the Chinese are part of us, and we are part of them, because we are all part of the same undivided whole; we are inextricably linked by the same energy, the same force of life.

Today the ordinary leader is weighed down by the burden of debt he incurred to finance a new state-of-the-art manufacturing plant in the United States. He simply cannot produce goods at a cost that leaves him room for a profit. He cannot raise his prices because a number of his competitors who had the presence, foresight, and intuition to move their manufacturing offshore are able to price their products at prices below his production costs. He has taken the only route open to him. He has declared bankruptcy.

The high-impact leader, on the other hand, recognized that the United States and China, and all other countries for that matter, are inextricably connected with each other and everything in our existence. She saw that nothing is separate and nothing is independent. As a student of the universe, she began sensing years ago a shifting of energies in our complex, adaptive system. She recognized that differences in language, culture, and politics, and geographic separation, are barriers created by the human mind and eminently surmountable. She observed a shifting political situation in China, one that was slowly embracing capitalism and its economic promise. She visited frequently and came to understand the power of over one billion highly energetic, resourceful, and intelligent people seeking to produce something. She noticed that their compensation needs and expectations were literally generations behind those of American workers. She watched as the country's leaders built an infrastructure to support production.

At the earliest opportunity, she began a dialogue with her Chinese brothers and sisters—yes, brothers and sisters—and began seeking ways they could each benefit from a relationship with each other. She found they needed jobs, training, education, and markets for goods they produced. She could fill those needs. She needed a lower cost, high-quality way of producing goods so that she could maintain or improve her profit margins and deliver more value to her shareholders. She found that the Chinese could fill her needs. As Bogart said in Casablanca, this was the "beginning of a beautiful friendship."

THE LEADERSHIP DASHBOARD

In the introduction, I presented the Leadership Dashboard as a tool for displaying leadership effectiveness, or the actual realization of the traits embodied by and functions performed by leaders. The high-impact leader achieves nearly 100 percent effectiveness in most or all traits and functions, while the ordinary leader achieves substantially less than 100 percent effectiveness in most or all areas. If you recall, I believe leaders on average are achieving less than 50 percent effectiveness across the Leadership Dashboard.

By definition, effective leaders are effective because people follow them. People follow them because they believe they possess the character traits of a leader and are capable of performing the functions of a leader. As discussed in the introduction, leaders historically have had certain advantages over the followers, such as superior knowledge, mobility, and communication. These advantages placed them closer—in the perception of those who followed—to what is real. And people followed their leaders—over the short- and medium-term—precisely because they perceived them to be closer to reality. In essence, leaders could "pull the wool over the eyes" of their followers. Today, however, these positional advantages are nearly gone. Everyone is on much more equal footing in terms of knowledge, mobility, and communication. To be effective, a leader must be closer to actual reality than those who follow. Otherwise, the leader will lack credibility and will have no followers.

If the historical positional advantages of a leader have nearly disappeared and we as effective leaders must be closer to actual reality than those whom we lead, how do we accomplish this? By being present. By being grounded in the present moment—the only reality there is—and aware of all dimensions of that reality. Presence is the new positional advantage of today's and tomorrow's leader. If you as a leader lack presence and grounding in true reality, then you will not be effective, and someone with presence and grounding will step forward and assume leadership.

Presence gives you the clarity of mind to define yourself accurately and thoroughly so that those who follow can have confidence that you will act consistently and with integrity. Presence gives you the ability to be forward thinking in a highly effective and efficient way because you are not mired in fears and because you know how to create a tomorrow that is an improvement over today. Presence gives you credibility because, understanding the interconnectedness of everyone in an undivided whole, you can only act in complete integrity. And, again, you are closer to actual reality—found in the present moment—than those you lead. Presence allows you to truly inspire other people because you are tapped into, and thus can draw others into, the energy that connects us all. Presence leaves no other option for you than to be people oriented because you understand that we are all part of each other in one undivided whole.

Presence provides you with abundant energy because you can easily identify sources of energy from which you can draw and energy drains you can avoid. Presence makes you more curious because you understand that everything is relevant and nothing can be ignored in an interconnected existence. Presence enables you to be highly courageous because you have minimized fear, a creation of the mind, and are intimately tuned into your intuition, a source of high-quality data. Presence means that your mind is much more focused and analytical, and your actions are much more organized, given that you are now a master at controlling your thoughts and eliminating worries of the future and regrets of the past.

Presence helps you build a values-based core because you are keenly aware of the needs of your team members, most of them not expressly disclosed by them, and the values that will address those needs and bind them to you, each other, and the organizational mission. Presence turns you into a font of new ideas and master formulator of visions because your mind, open and relaxed as it is, is more fertile than ever before. Presence allows you to build a plan because you see with stunning clarity —unobstructed by fears, regrets, and emotion—the best path from where you are now to where you want to be.

Presence enables you to engage a team because, grounded in reality, you know the type of people needed, the way to inspire them and secure their commitment, the way to communicate with them, and the way to reward them. Presence shows you how to build a responsive structure that best serves the organizational objectives and the people in that structure in an existence where change is the only constant. Presence allows you to create a high degree of accountability because you have created an inspirational environment of complete personal responsibility, free of blame or disownment. Finally, in the end and as a result of all of the foregoing, presence ultimately enables you to produce results.

Presence, I believe, is the personal energy—the key internal driver— that facilitates all traits and functions of a leader. In fact, I believe it is the only one that underlies every trait and function. Moreover, it underlies each of the other internal drivers discussed in the remainder of this book. As such, it is the first, most important, and the most potent step toward high-impact leadership.

But at the same time, presence alone is not enough. It is too amorphous to completely enable the very specific character traits and functions of a leader. It gets you part of the way there, but not all the way. On the Leadership Dashboard in figure 1.1, we'll assume that presence gets you 50 percent of the way toward being a high-impact leader. In reality, this is completely arbitrary. For instance, presence may be a huge factor in one's ability to be self-defined, and only a minor factor in another's. My point is that, based on my experience, presence or awareness is a critical component of the traits and functions traditionally ascribed to the high-impact leader. And while presence, I believe, gets you farther than most leaders toward high-impact leadership, why not optimize? Just going part of the way there is senseless. If we are going to attempt something, let's go all the way. Going all the way requires seven other, more specific, drivers or energies covered in the next seven chapters.

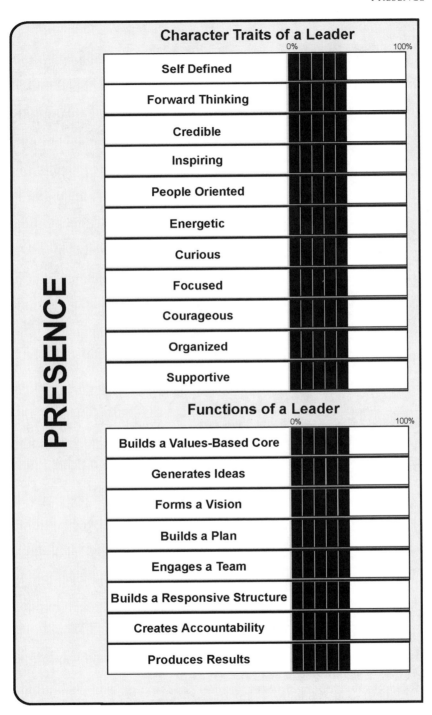

FIGURE 1.1

CHAPTER 2

OPENNESS

The Second Driver of the
High-Impact Leader

Openness is the willingness to consider every element of "what is." As you move toward a state of presence, you take a huge step toward accessing and developing the driver of openness. In a purely present state, there is nothing but openness. There is only expansiveness and receptivity. There is no resistance. There are no boundaries, restrictions, or restraints. In this chapter, you'll come to understand openness as your natural state and learn how to hone this driver to become a curious, forward-thinking high-impact leader who generates a wealth of ideas and forms powerful visions for your organization.

> *Openness* **is the willingness to consider every element of "what is."**

BORN OPEN, THEN BOXED UP

You came into this world wide open to absolutely everything. You couldn't absorb enough. You listened to everything. You heard everything. You tasted everything you could get into your mouth. You smelled everything. You touched everything in every conceivable way. You saw everything. As you developed during your earliest years, your mind knew no boundaries. Why this? Why that? Why not that? What if this? What if that?

But soon after birth, society began to build a box around you. You started to close up. Your parents, siblings, caregivers, teachers, friends, and strangers all helped with the construction. Perhaps one parent told you, "It isn't nice to cough without covering your mouth." The other might have said, "Dogs are smelly and dirty." Your sister may have said, "Stay off of my bed." Perhaps your brother said, "Only boys can play baseball." Your day-care provider might have said, "Lower your voice," and your teacher, "There are right answers and wrong answers. Right answers are good, and wrong answers are bad. Right answers will lead to success, and wrong answers will lead to failure." A friend might have said, "You'll look stupid if you wear short hair." Perhaps a stranger gave you a nasty look when you screamed loudly while walking down the street.

You probably pitched in, innocently enough, in the construction of the box. Maybe you fell off your bike, scraped your knee, and thought, "I need to ride more slowly and be more careful." Maybe when you tried to throw a football, it popped out of your hand and fell to the ground, and you thought, "This is too hard. I can't throw a football." Maybe you saw all your friends wearing bell-bottom pants and thought, "I have to wear bell-bottoms to be accepted by my friends."

Within a few years, the box was largely built. And for the average person, the walls and ceiling moved closer each day after that. By the time you became an adult, if you are average, the box was pretty tight around you. And every day after that, chances are, it only got tighter. You became more and more fixed in your beliefs, habits, reactions, and behaviors. One day, if you are average, you woke up and found some or all of the following to be true for you:

YOU WANT TO BE RIGHT. You heard your teachers loudly and clearly. There are "right" ways and "wrong" ways. There are "right" answers and "wrong" answers. If you do things the right way, you will succeed and if you do them the wrong way, you will fail.

YOU DON'T WANT TO FAIL. Success is good and failure is bad. You will suffer if you fail. So you may be afraid of taking "unreasonable" risks.

YOU LIKE RULES. Look at our society. There is law upon law, and regulation upon regulation. You do the same at work and at home. With no rules, how would you know how to act?

YOU LIKE ORDER. You may embrace routines and traditions. You may fear chaos. You may fear the unexpected, the irrational, and the random.

YOU DIFFERENTIATE AND JUDGE. If you want so badly to be right, and you love rules and order, you may differentiate and judge excessively. You may put everything and everyone into positive and negative categories. Your need to be right might make you put most of that which is outside of you and different from you in negative categories. Then you may condescend because you can't escape your fear that maybe you're not right after all. You think that maybe if you declare often enough that others are wrong, it will actually make you right.

YOU SEEK THE BEST. Most of the time, you seek out and then become attached to the "best" of everything. You are infatuated with the best practice, product, service, idea, and strategy.

YOU ACCEPT ADEQUACY. The remainder of the time, you accept that which works adequately for you. If it ain't broke, you don't fix it.

YOU ARE EMBARRASSED ABOUT DAYDREAMING AND FANTASY. You may feel that letting your mind wander is wasteful. You may feel that you have to be active and moving to be productive and valuable. You may be ashamed about your fantasies and dreams.

YOU ARE REALISTIC AND LOGICAL. Perhaps this is the only way you can make sense of things, and you may feel that you have to make sense of things to survive.

YOU LIMIT YOUR HUMAN INTERACTION. Other people are different. They may be bad. They may be dangerous. You might say, "I won't talk too much to them. I'll build fences. If I can find other like-minded folks, then we'll form a club, make rules, and exclude people who don't think like us."

RESISTING OPENNESS

If some or all of the characteristics above seem familiar, you may have learned to resist openness. Resistance is basically a lack of openness. If you are like most people, you resist. You resist ideas other than your own. You resist the unknown. You resist taking risks. You resist operating without order. You resist breaking the rules. You resist human interaction and anything that confuses you. You may even resist dreaming.

When you resist something, however, you give energy to that which you resist. You give it fuel and keep it alive. What you resist, persists. And, of course, you lose some of your own valuable energy in the process. You become weaker and feel more pain.

Resistance in a leader seriously compromises his or her ability to embody the character traits and perform the functions of a high-impact leader. Specifically, the lack of openness makes it very difficult to be forward thinking and curious, or to generate ideas and develop a plan for the future. The future is too wide open and unknown, so he or she shrinks into—and spends his or her time in—what is familiar. The familiar, of course, is that which has already been experienced.

EXERCISE:
FORCE VS. RESISTANCE

In many of my seminars, we do an exercise that demonstrates the negative effect of resistance so vividly that participants often tell me years later that they have never forgotten the experience and apply it daily to their lives. As a leader, whenever I am inclined to resist a new idea, event, or condition, I think of this exercise and find that my resistance quickly dissipates. The exercise calls for a partner, so you'll have to enlist a friend or family member. Assume the role of the Resister and ask your partner to be the Force.

STEP 1: FACE OFF

Stand facing each other about a foot apart, but offset so that the right shoulder of your partner, the Force, directly faces your right shoulder. Plant your feet firmly and don't move them during the exercise. Interlock your right hand with the right hand of the Force and hold the joined hands a few inches above your shoulders.

STEP 2: RESIST

On the count of three, the Force pushes as hard as he or she can against your right hand, and you, the Resister, use all of your strength to stop the Force's hand. You can feel the tension in the room. Force and Resister, your partner and you, are engaged in battle. The likely result of the battle is that you, the Resister, are thrown off balance, lose your stance, and awkwardly stumble backward or to the side.

STEP 3: GO WITH THE FLOW

Take a few breaths and prepare to do the exercise again. This time, however, offer no resistance whatsoever. On the count of three, allow your hand to go where the Force's hand takes it. You'll see that it will go straight over your shoulder, while you remain firmly planted on the ground. This step should take about a second.

What did you experience? Did you notice a difference between the two steps? For instance, in step 2, did you as the Resister expend and lose a great amount of energy over an extended period in the act of resisting? In step 3, did you lose any energy, or did the force flow by you? What about control? When did you feel more in control—when you were resisting or not resisting?

BREAK OUT OF THE BOX

Openness was defined at the beginning of this chapter as the willingness to consider every element of "what is." As such, openness is a function of choice, intent, and practice. You simply have to choose to "break out of the box," apply your intention, and take action.

There are many ways to break out of the box, reduce resistance, and build the driver of openness that will fuel what you are and do as a leader. The objective is to exercise the "input" valve in your brain. For most people, the input valve is essentially closed. For a leader, this is a fatal condition. Your organization expects you to generate or at least identify the best ideas, formulate the optimal vision for the organization, build a plan for attaining that vision, and build a responsive, flexible organization to execute the plan. To be successful, you must be able to identify as many connections and see as many alternatives as you possibly can. You must be wide open. The exercises below will help you immensely.

Of all exercises designed to enhance openness, I believe meditation, described in chapter 1, is the most powerful. Ultimately we are looking to change a condition of resistance, close-mindedness, and stubborn or unconscious attachment to ideas or beliefs. The first step in the process of change is awareness of the current condition and the need for change. The best technique for increasing awareness, or consciousness, is meditation. It gets your mind and thoughts out of the way and allows you to experience and comprehend what is real.

Some other favorite exercises of mine for increasing awareness and developing openness are the following:

EXERCISE:
THE SCRAMBLE

This is a simple but powerful exercise for opening your mind that you can do anywhere and anytime. In your mind, start changing everything you perceive. If you sit down in an airplane and see the notice on the seat in front of you that says "Fasten Seat Belt While Seated," think of fastening the seat belt while standing. Then think about not fastening the seat belt while seated. Then think about standing on your head in the seat and fastening the seat belt. You get the idea. When driving down the freeway, imagine driving in reverse. Imagine all the other cars driving in reverse. Imagine them upside down. Imagine them flying. Imagine the freeway going straight up into the sky. Imagine it going down through the earth. Imagine people riding on the outside of their vehicles. Again, you get the idea. Who needs Dr. Timothy Leary's LSD when mind expansion can be had at any time, at no cost, with neither side effects nor the risk of overdose?

EXERCISE:
PATTERN BREAKS AND BELIEF SWAPS

Think about everything you ordinarily do, then do it differently. If you always awake at six with an alarm, try not setting an alarm and waking up naturally. If you always have cereal for breakfast, have a couple of eggs instead, or skip breakfast. If you always follow one route to work, try another route, even though it may be longer. If you always arrive at work at a certain time, arrive at another time. If you always park in a certain space at work, park next to that space, or across the lot. Or take a cab. Or walk. If you're not a vegetarian, try being one. If you are a vegetarian, have some meat. Fast for a few days. If you run for exercise, try cycling, walking, or yoga instead. If you rarely read, read. If you always watch television, don't watch television. If you rarely watch television, watch it a lot for a few days. Sleep in a different bed.

Then swap your beliefs. If you are politically liberal, try thinking like a conservative for a day and try to see everything through a conservative's eyes. If you are a conservative, try being a liberal. If you believe in gun control, spend a day making a case for no restrictions on weapons. If you are a staunch Catholic, live a day as an atheist. Be a Buddhist. If you are Jewish, try thinking and behaving like a Catholic for a day.

Following patterns and adhering to beliefs are like racing on a small, steeply banked racetrack. When you are in it, you are blind to everything outside of it. The longer you stay in it, the blinder you become, that is, the less aware you are of the environment outside of the track. Breaking patterns and experimenting with different beliefs helps you to remove your blind spots and to become more aware of the reality—what truly exists—around you. Again, today's leaders must be closer to what is real than those they lead, or they won't lead effectively for long.

EXERCISE:
TAKE A "SENSORY SPRING BREAK"

What did a lot of us do on college spring break? We broke out of our school routines and crossed a lot of our normal boundaries. We may have drunk too much, tried some new substances, flashed our breasts or bottoms to members of the opposite sex, or even had sex with people we hardly knew. Actually, I never did these things. Unfortunately, I had to work to earn enough money to finish out the term. But I have heard a lot of spring-break stories. And I think we all need to break out of our sensory routines in much the same way. Taste new things. Go out for Nepalese food if you have never had it before. Listen to new music. If you are a classical music lover, go out and buy a Busta Rhymes CD and listen to it over and over again. Smell new things. Smell everything you can for a day. Smell every flower, every tree, every book, every garbage can, and every person who will let you. Feel new things. If you hate the feel of not bathing every day, go camping for a week and don't wash yourself. Get a massage. Stand on your head. See new things. Buy a magnifying glass and start looking at things near to you even more closely. Buy a pair of binoculars and start looking at distant things more closely.

EXERCISE:
BREAK A RULE

Don't get yourself thrown in jail or take unreasonable physical or economic risks, but start breaking some rules. Hop over a fence into a gated subdivision and take a walk. Walk into a restaurant with bare feet and ask for a seat. Be late for work. People will almost certainly step forward when they can and tell you that you are breaking the rules, and that's okay. Politely thank them. If they start getting really irritated or threatening you, it's probably best to back off. They just don't understand that you are in the process of liberating your mind and soul. One thing that often happens with this exercise is that you find yourself justifying the rule you want to break. You "overthink" the exercise. Don't do it. Just break the rule and see how it feels.

EXERCISE:
PRACTICE SPONTANEOUS RANDOMNESS

Do completely senseless things and then ponder them for a purpose. Maybe you'll find one and maybe you won't, but they are bound to open you up. Get up for no reason and walk outside, down to the corner, and back. Why did you do that? Maybe you saw something you had never seen before and it gave you a new idea or raised a new question. Maybe you ran into an old acquaintance. Maybe you met someone new. Maybe it was a signal that you were losing traction with whatever you were working on and needed to go in a new direction. Buy a book on fly-fishing, even though you have no interest in it. Open to a random page, and study what is written on it. Why? Who knows? But I guarantee your mind will open and some beneficial cognition will arise.

EXERCISE:
BE WEIRD

Large parts of the box around us are the standards of other people. We understand what they will accept from us and what they will reject, and we act accordingly. But "accordingly" usually means what they will accept. How about changing, on occasion, "accordingly" to what will stun them, what will make them uncomfortable, what they will reject, or what they will mock? How do you do this? It's simple: look to the example of an eighteen-month-old baby. Scream in joy as you walk down a busy sidewalk. Make funny faces to strangers. Talk loud in a library. Demand loudly what you want. Throw food. Rub it all over your face. Scream in pain when you are hurt. Cry. Clap. Sit down on the ground and study a bug.

EXERCISE:
FAIL

Look for ways to experience failure. Only through failure do we grow, and we just aren't letting ourselves fail enough. We are stunting our growth. As a leader or prospective leader, you likely don't fail very often. How about trying something new? Go run a marathon. Try out for a local theater production. Take the most challenging class you can think of. Buy a canvas and some paint and try to paint a masterpiece work of art. Start to get comfortable out of the range of success.

THE "BOUNDARIES" OF OPENNESS

Many people ask, "How can I lead if I am so open? Won't I be floating all over the place? Won't I lack definition and conviction? If leadership is about producing an effect and meeting objectives, how do I do that by casting myself adrift?" Those are great questions.

The answer is that you can lead, and lead very well, with openness. You won't be floating all over the place, lacking definition and conviction. The openness I espouse is within and around the traits and functions of leadership. In other words, there are boundaries on openness in the context of leadership. The leader who has mastered openness still must—with firmness, conviction, and solid grounding—perform the traditional leadership functions described in the introduction: build a values-based core, generate ideas, form a vision, build a plan, engage a team, build a responsive structure, create accountability, and produce results. Because he or she is open, however, he or she builds a better core, generates more and better ideas, forms a better and more valuable vision, builds a more efficient plan, engages a more talented

> The leader who has mastered openness still must—with firmness, conviction, and solid grounding—perform the traditional leadership functions: build a values-based core, generate ideas, form a vision, build a plan, engage a team, build a responsive structure, create accountability, and produce results.

team, builds a more responsive structure, creates stronger accountability, and produces better results.

The High-Impact Leader Empowered by Openness: Tom Anderson and Chris DeWolfe

Openness is the fuel that produced one of the most success-ful Internet sites today. If you asked most "in the know" people about how to launch a social networking site, they would tell you to build content that was already demand-proven by other sites and employ a structure that works well in other sites or, at the very least, a structure that has been validated by market research. In other words, go with what you know, with what is safe, with what is defined.

And if the founders of MySpace.com, today's hottest site for the crowd between sixteen and twenty-four years old, had done that, they would have produced a nice little site, with a nice little flow of traffic, and a nice little stream of advertising revenue. But instead, Tom Anderson and Chris DeWolfe just opened up to the universe. They ignored the boundaries of what is known, safe, and defined. They asked themselves how com-munities of any type grow and flourish, and came up with the now obvious answer that communities grow the way they want to grow. And the more control participants have in their com-munity, the more attracted they are to it, and the more time they spend in it.

So they launched MySpace.com in late 2003, leaving it to community members to build whatever content they wanted. The company merely provided tools needed by members to establish a presence and participate fully in the community, the infrastructure needed to make the content best serve commu-nity members. In less than two years, the company had over twenty million registered users and was attracting larger adver-tising revenues than all but a handful of sites on the Internet. Rupert Murdoch's News Corporation bought its parent company for $580 million in July 2005. By September 2006, less than thirty-six months after its launch, the site had one hundred million registered users, and ranked second only to Yahoo! in page views, with one billion daily. All because these guys were open, not attached to an idea of how things "should" be, and didn't try to force anything on anyone (Sellers 2006).

THE LEADERSHIP DASHBOARD

As an open leader, your vision of possibilities is not obscured. You can hunt down and devour as much information as is available. While it may sound exhausting, in fact it is energizing. Finding and understanding the data and connections all around you becomes addictive. Ideas flow from you because you can see connections—possibilities—hidden to others. Visions flow from you. Others will follow because you see more than they do. You are closer to reality and they see that.

Figure 2.1, the Leadership Dashboard, demonstrates graphically how openness is a key source of energy empowering you as a leader to exemplify many of the character traits and execute the many functions of the high-impact leader described in the introduction. It shows that openness, fueled itself by the driver of presence, enables you to:

BE FORWARD THINKING. The closed mind, afraid of the unknown, naturally dwells in the past, which is largely known. The open mind naturally ponders the future and possibilities. With openness, you will start envisioning bolder, more exciting possibilities for you and your organization.

BE CURIOUS. Again, without the fear that drives a closed mind, you will seek the new and unknown.

GENERATE IDEAS. You will be a thought leader, identifying new associations and connections, and originating new ways of thinking and doing things.

FORM A VISION. Unbounded by fear, flowing with ideas, and thinking forward, you'll be highly effective at formulating optimal, achievable, and valuable organizational objectives.

The driver of openness will also fuel, albeit to a lesser extent, your ability to:

BE CREDIBLE. Openness will enhance your team members' confidence in your abilities and character because they will see the congruency between your lack of fear of the unknown future and your role as the one who will lead them to a better future.

BE INSPIRING. Openness contributes to your ability to identify the common purpose in your organization, and then articulate your vision in a way that your team members see themselves as an integral part of it.

BE PEOPLE ORIENTED. In my experience, an open mind leads to an open heart, and ultimately a genuine love for people.

BE ENERGETIC. Once over your fear of the unknown, openness and the possibilities it reveals are invigorating.

ENGAGE A TEAM. People migrate toward the fearless, those with the exciting ideas, and those with the most energy. Openness enhances your ability to recruit, engage, and inspire people to realize the vision you have created for your organization.

BUILD A RESPONSIVE STRUCTURE. Openness allows you to envision and create a permeable, flexible structure that is highly adaptive to rapidly changing conditions.

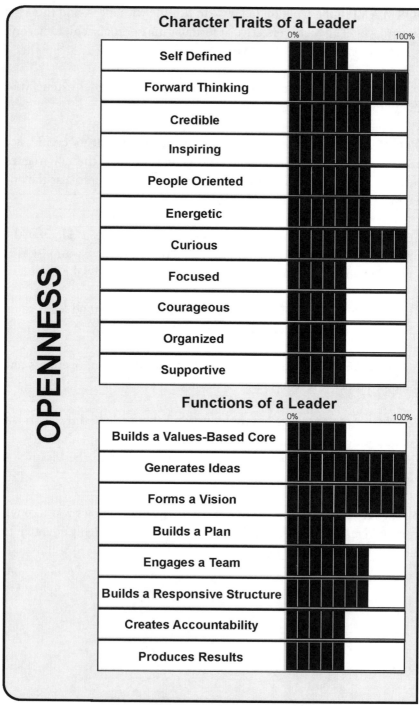

FIGURE 2.1

CHAPTER 3

CLARITY
The Third Driver of the High-Impact Leader

Clarity is a high degree of clearness, or transparency, in one's thoughts, behaviors, and actions. When you consider some of the critical traits and functions necessary for high-impact leadership—things like being self-defined and people oriented, creating an organizational core based on human values, and engaging people to execute an organizational plan—you'll likely see how important it is that a leader have a high degree of clarity in his or her thoughts, emotions, and behavior. The leader who is positive thinking will be more effective than the leader who is mired in worry, distrust, or negative or critical thought. The leader who is emotionally stable will be more effective than the one who struggles with envy, anger, impatience, or shame. The leader who is steady in his or her behavior will be far more effective than the one who lies, cheats, has destructive addictions, or abuses staff with rage, condescension, or criticism.

If leadership is ultimately about transforming personal energies into interpersonal

> *Clarity* **is a high degree of clearness, or transparency, in one's thoughts, behaviors, and actions.**

results, then clarity of thought, emotion, and behavior can be thought of as the grease that facilitates the process: the healthier the thought, emotion, and behavior of the leader, the more efficient the transformation and the better the results.

Unfortunately, in my experience, clarity of thought, emotion, and behavior is largely lacking among leaders. Not that leaders are less healthy in this respect than nonleaders, but their lack of health affects more lives just by virtue of their being leaders. Leaders may have gone to business school, may have more industry experience, or may know more in specific areas than anyone else, but it's likely they never took a course called "Cleaning Out Your Emotional and Behavioral Baggage So That You Can Work Effectively with People and Thoroughly Engage Them in the Pursuit of the Organization's Mission." It is incumbent upon you as a leader, however, to master the material of that course on your own. It is often a painful process, but the energy that is liberated in the process, and the direct increase in your effectiveness as a leader, leave no question about its value. I would also argue that you have a fiduciary responsibility to achieve clarity for the simple fact that people are following you. It is one thing to allow distortion in your thoughts, emotions, and behavior to negatively affect your own life. It is another thing, and just plain wrong, to allow it to negatively affect the lives of those who follow you and the organization whose stewardship with which you have been entrusted. For example, the rage, condescension, and silent treatment that are used, intentionally or not, by some leaders are forms of abuse and undermine everything else a leader might try to accomplish.

The more present you are, the more you will be aware of where your thoughts, emotions, or behaviors are distorted. In a purely present state, there is no distortion. You are clear in your thinking, emoting, and behaving. Few people, however, are purely present all of the time, or even most of the time. But as you understand and move toward that condition, you become more aware of where distortion lies. Awareness, of course, is the first and hardest step toward solving a problem. In this case, awareness of distortion is the first step toward achieving clarity. In this chapter, you'll come to understand clarity as a powerful driver that fuels your ability to be a self-defined, people-oriented high-impact leader with the ability to build a values-based core in your organization and engage a team in your mission.

THE PERSONA AND THE SHADOW

In this chapter, I'll use the concept of persona and shadow as a framework for addressing clarity of thought, emotion, and behavior. Scholars credit Carl Jung, the famous Swiss psychiatrist, as among the first to talk about the persona and shadow, the two parts of our personality, in a scientific context (Zweig and Abrams 1991, xvi–xxv). The *persona*, which derives from the Latin word meaning "mask," is the appearance you present to the world: the face you wear, your social roles, how you express yourself. Your persona is ever-changing. You consciously change your persona to fit the situation.

The *shadow* consists of elements of yourself that you don't want others to see and of which, often, you are not even conscious. It includes tendencies and desires that you dislike or that someone disliked in you, usually at an early age. It includes parts of yourself that you reject, consciously or unconsciously, as incompatible with your persona and, often, that are contrary to social standards.

The repressed traits of the shadow can be negative or positive. For instance, I might have been a talented dancer as a young child, but suppressed the quality after being taunted by other kids who considered it an activity restricted to girls. Those qualities, as well as my fears around expressing them, were deposited into my shadow. Ironically, the shadow, which we often feel negatively about when we recognize it, can also be seen as a gift.

The shadow contains at least two gifts if you dig into it deeply enough. First, you will find those positive traits—for instance, creativity, sexuality, assertiveness—that were buried in your shadow many years ago. How many people say, "I'm not really creative—I could never be an artist"? I said that for most of my life and then one day decided that maybe, in fact, I was creative and could be an artist, and it was all buried in my shadow. Indeed, I discovered it and became a successful painter.

Second, you will find those negative traits that undermine your personal contentment, your relationships, and your effectiveness as a leader. Once identified—and identifying them is the most difficult step—you can work with them so that they no longer undermine your life.

Let's take a look now at three different people—Ellen, Bill, and David—and see how their shadows undermined their lives and their leadership effectiveness.

DR. JEKYLL OR MR. HYDE?

Ellen had a resumé that dwarfed those of just about anyone with whom she ever crossed paths: Ivy League undergraduate and postgraduate degrees, and all the academic honors one person could amass. She served several years as the right-hand person to one of the world's great industrialists, participating in meetings with heads of state and managing transactions among the world's top companies. She went on to lead major corporations. Her persona was quiet, warm, gentle, humble, and curious. Her shadow, however, emerged after several months in every professional situation in which she was involved. She was extraordinarily controlling, abusive to those who interfered with her control, condescending to most everyone, and dishonest with almost everyone. While she hid these traits very well from her board members, the folks with the ability to fire her, no one who ever worked with her on a day-to-day basis for any period of time liked her, and most sought the nearest exit whenever she appeared.

Bill was an accomplished chief executive who ran one of the nation's largest retail companies. Armed with an MBA from one of the top business schools, twenty-five years in the industry, a warm personality, and an extraordinary amount of confidence, he performed a difficult job very well. His persona was that of a sincere, highly confident, ethical, values-based family man. Hiding in his shadow, however, was a sex addict. Married to the same woman for twenty-five years, with five children, he could not stop himself from engaging in everything from one-night stands in distant cities to yearlong affairs with employees. As time went on, everyone except his wife—partners, employees, clients—learned of his habits. His ability to lead suffered substantially as his fundamental lack of integrity became evident.

You already know a bit about the third person, David—that's me. For years, I seemed successful in almost every respect. I had a law degree and an MBA from top schools, and a track record as a successful lawyer, then investment banker, then corporate executive. I had a wife and two sons, with whom I seemed very happy. I earned a lot of money, had a beautiful home in the California Wine Country, several nice cars, and a healthy investment portfolio. My persona was that of a hardworking, personable but tough, ethical, and intelligent professional. My shadow, however, was almost insufferably insecure. In reality, I worked so hard because I was terrified of failing. I was impatient with people who I felt were not working as hard as I was. I resisted change. I was highly judgmental of others. I had an anger that was always active just below the surface and occasionally erupted in rage. I was not in love with my wife and emotionally abused her by criticizing and controlling her. As a leader, I suffered because people were not clear about exactly who I was and what I stood for. I preached about the need for a values-based core, which included a respect for one's life outside of work, but in reality had an unhappy, neglected personal life. I either alienated or was an enigma to just enough people to prevent full engagement with my team.

Do you see any of these behaviors in yourself or in leaders you know or have known? Do you see other behaviors that are just as harmful? If you do, I'm certain your (or their) ability to lead is seriously compromised. Because recognizing and understanding the shadow is so important, let's look a little closer at this elusive psychological phenomenon.

THE LONG BAG TRAILING BEHIND YOU

In a wonderful book entitled *A Little Book on the Human Shadow*, the renowned poet Robert Bly (1988, 17–25) metaphorically described the shadow as a long bag you drag behind yourself. You came into the world with a 360-degree personality. You were a full, indeed overflowing, ball of energy. Bit by bit, little incident by little incident, you began slicing off parts of your personality and throwing them in the bag: "Don't yell so loud." "Don't get angry at your brother." "It isn't nice to not share." "Don't ask so many questions." "It is none of your business." If you are a boy, "Only girls dance." If a girl, "Playing baseball is not 'ladylike.'" And this continued at least through high school and all the social paranoia of that time. Parents, teachers, friends, and strangers all helped you take slices off of yourself and throw them into the long bag behind you. And you, of course, helped your friends, children, and students fill up their long bags.

So you ended up, in your early twenties, as a very "nice" person, with a thin, light slice of yourself visible to everyone else, even your loved ones, and a long bag filled up with all the parts of yourself that influential people in your life didn't want you to display. The bigger the bag, the more energy it contains, and the less positive energy you have in your persona. If you are male, you may have put your feminine side—your intuition, sensitivity, nurturing—in the bag. If female, you may have put your masculine side—your aggressiveness, anger, appetite for risk—in the bag. You may have thrown your sexuality, creativity, and expressiveness in there as well. Well, that's a whole lot of energy trapped in that bag and you are pretty seriously handicapped if you can't access it. Your energy is depleted in two ways. First, you expend energy in suppressing what is in your shadow. Second, you expend energy in maintaining a persona that is not aligned with your shadow.

But it's worse than just depleted energy. The energies trapped in the long bag—your shadow—get hostile over time. They don't like the fact they have been rejected. They fester and they lash out at inopportune times. They undermine your persona. You have seen it countless times in yourself and others, but you may not have known what you were seeing and the effect it was having on you. Think, for example, about the previously serene, good-natured person, perhaps even yourself, who all of a sudden rages. We've all seen this happen, and it shocked us. The energies trapped in their bag, perhaps shame or envy, were hidden for so long that they literally exploded.

IDENTIFYING SHADOW TRAITS

So how do you tap into your shadow? How do you get into that long bag behind you? How do you start identifying what really exists deep within you—what you avoid showing to other people—and come to terms with it? How do you come to terms in a way that the negative traits do not hinder your ability to relate to others and to live a deeply contented life, and that the positive traits are brought into the light so that you can optimize your life? In short, how do you achieve clarity of thought, emotion, and behavior?

A practice of presence, discussed in chapter 1, is the best way to start. The more present you are, the more you are aware of yourself. The shadow represents a huge imbalance within you. In essence, it is the tension between real and unreal, truth and honesty, the hidden and the exposed.

In *Your Golden Shadow*, William A. Miller (1989, 51–62) provides some excellent suggestions for identifying your shadow traits. Among them are the following:

SOLICIT FEEDBACK FROM OTHERS

When one is blind to something, usually only another person can shine light on the subject in a way that illuminates it for us. As threatening and as painful as this may be, there may be no better method for identifying one's shadow traits than soliciting input from someone in your life who can communicate directly, honestly, and without fear of repercussion in a personal relationship. This may be a spouse, a friend, a coworker, manager, or professional therapist. If you have any doubt about the validity of the feedback, ask another person. If they give the same feedback, you have probably identified a shadow trait or traits. A strong sign that you have hit on something is if every fiber in your body wants to argue the point and prove how wrong their observation is.

EXERCISE:
THE TOUGHEST EVALUATION YOU'LL EVER GET

A lack of clarity in your thoughts, emotions, and behavior will seriously undermine your ability as a leader to be self-defined and people-oriented, and to build a values-based core and engage a team in the pursuit of your organizational mission. Thus, it is critical to identify where clarity is lacking or, in "shadow speak," where shadow traits are undermining your behavior.

In this exercise, you will seek clarity about your behavior. In particular, you'll ask someone to help you identify traits that may be part of your shadow. Find a person who knows you well—spouse, friend, coworker, manager, professional therapist—and ask him or her to complete the worksheet below. Copies of the worksheet are available for download at www.thesourceofleadership.com/downloads.

This would be a difficult exercise if you answered it yourself, but having someone else do it is even more difficult—but also extraordinarily beneficial. To gain the full benefit of the exercise, make and honor a commitment to be open to the answers the responder gives. Do not argue with the responder, defend yourself, or take any retaliatory action. If you can do this, it will be one of the most life-altering exercises you ever undertake.

My Behavior

Your Name: _____

Instructions: Please place a check mark in the appropriate column indicating how frequently the person named above exhibits each of the behaviors listed below:

	Never	Occasionally	Often
Gets angry at others			
Gives the silent treatment			
Makes negative comments			
Raises voice with others			
Thinks negative thoughts			
Gossips			
Criticizes others			
Fears others are against him/her			
Attempts to control others			

Sees the worst in people			
Seeks revenge			
Is contentious with others			
Speaks of taking revenge			
Acts overly competitive			
Is impatient			
Condescends			
Is moody			
Makes threats			
Acts passively aggressive			
Speaks with excessive sarcasm			
Avoids taking risks			
Does not cooperate with others			
Physically abuses others			
Acts like a victim			
Reacts negatively to criticism			
Always arrives late			
Lacks empathy for others			
Does not honor commitments			
Acts jealous or possessive			
Sulks or pouts			
Needs constant support from others			
Withholds approval of others			
Has an addiction			
Procrastinates			
Gets embarrassed often			
Seems to feel shame			
Embarrasses others often			
Seems to feel inadequate			

SCORING. I believe the ideal is a worksheet that shows a number of behaviors marked "Never" and some marked "Occasionally." We are, after all, human. I don't think I have yet met the person who would have

"Never" marked throughout. Any behavior marked "Often" indicates a lack of clarity in your behavior, or shadow traits that are negatively affecting your behavior, that need to be addressed. If many behaviors are marked "Occasionally," that usually indicates a lack of clarity and undermining shadow traits as well.

If you don't like the answers that are given for you, consider it an immense gift. Your dislike is a clear message that you have some cleaning up to do. Most people never face their own behavior squarely and live lives of quiet—or sometimes raging—discontent. Again, awareness of a problem or issue is the first and hardest step in the change process. In this case, awareness of the distortion is the first step in achieving clarity.

EXCESSIVE EMOTION OR OVERREACTION TO BEHAVIORS IN OTHERS

We all are aware of behaviors in others that displease us. But there are some behaviors that really get under our skin. When this happens, we have identified part of our shadow. Yes, those things we most loathe in others are buried inside us.

In my younger years, I would get extremely mad at motorists who drove impatiently. As they would tailgate others, speed excessively, and cut people off, my blood would boil. If I had a chance, I would do what I could to foil their behavior. I'd often "flip them the bird," all the while decrying what demons they were.

As I became more present, I was finally prepared to dig deeply and honestly into my shadow. Among the multitudes of traits I discovered, I found that I was extremely impatient on the road. I got a lot of speeding tickets. I would tailgate others when they were going too slow, which was often the speed limit. I thought all drivers were less skillful than I was, and that their schedules were less important than mine. People very close to me had told me about this in years past, but I defended my behavior vigorously. Shadow traits have strong survival instincts, and this one did not want to die. Once pulled from the shadow, however, and exposed to the light—that is, when I admitted my behavior to myself and talked with others about it—it was amazing how quickly its energy dissipated. I am grateful to say that after many years as a shadow "road rager," I am now very much a civil and calm driver. I haven't had a ticket in years. The real proof is that those drivers that used to really enrage me no longer ignite any emotional charge in me.

A wonderful, and difficult, exercise suggested by Miller (1989) is to write down those traits in others that really irk you. Not mildly irk you, but make you extremely upset. Spend some time with those and honestly search for those traits inside yourself. They are almost certainly within you, in your shadow. If arrogant people enrage you, search for arrogance in your shadow. Do you have an arrogant side to you? If you can't find the trait inside yourself, go back to the exercise above, The Toughest Evaluation You'll Ever Get, and solicit the input of others who might know you better than you do.

EXAMINE YOUR "SLIPS"

Look for slips of tongue, slips of behavior, and situations where your behavior was misperceived. Once I heard a plumber, someone I thought I knew reasonably well and who always seemed to be a very nice, gentle, caring man, respond to his new assistant in an unexpectedly vehement way. When his assistant asked if they were going to take the day off to celebrate Martin Luther King Jr. Day, the plumber told his assistant that he was going to "work extra hard" on that day. As his assistant sat in silence, not knowing what to say, the plumber quickly changed the subject. I noticed his face was blushing. I suspect that his shadow possessed some racism, and yet one would never detect it in his persona.

For many years, my rage was deeply embedded in my shadow. Every now and then, I would have a "behavioral slip" and erupt, yell, and say mean things. People would remark that "it was so out of character." Well, it was very much in my shadow's character, though my persona did a very good job of hiding it most of the time.

DREAMS, DAYDREAMS, AND FANTASIES

We all dream, daydream, and fantasize. We do these a lot. Pay attention to figures of the same sex who appear in your dreams or daydreams, to which you respond with fear, dislike, or disgust. They may be displaying your shadow traits.

I had a client once who told me he used to have dreams in which a certain Hollywood movie actor treated women in degrading ways. In subsequent therapy, he learned that, in fact, he had long been degrading to women, both in his personal and professional life, in subtle and sometimes not-so-subtle ways. It is likely that his behavior was a result of his anger at being abandoned by his mother at a very young age.

WORKING WITH SHADOW TRAITS

Every person has a persona and a shadow. Your emotional health is a function of the extent to which you acknowledge your shadow traits, are able to understand how they affect your persona, and can mitigate their negative features while exploiting the positive ones. The more shadow traits are made conscious, the less they can dominate. But the shadow is an integral part of our nature, and it can never be simply eliminated.

The healthiest person has a rather mild shadow and is very familiar with it and how it operates. The unhealthiest person has a huge shadow and is completely unconscious to its existence. Most of us are somewhere between the extremes. Most of us are aware of some elements of our shadow, unconscious to others, and have built only a few of the many bridges between the two that are necessary for true contentment and a harmonious life. Sherry, for instance, the chief operating officer of a small company, has some significant shadow traits that developed in her "military brat" upbringing. Her parents were extremely strict, and she developed obsessive-compulsive behaviors that were not severe but which negatively impacted her personal and professional relationships. In particular, she had a tendency to micromanage her children and her team members. Over time, with some counseling, she became very aware of her behavioral tendencies and was able to learn healthier ways to act. Her parents' occasional rages, however, had instilled shame in her that made her rage in the same way on occasion at her children and team members. Unfortunately, she is still blind to this issue and, as a result, struggles in her parental relationship and with effectively engaging her team.

The identification of shadow traits is very difficult. They have, as I said earlier, strong survival instincts. They are threatened by the light. They thrive by staying hidden in the dark. Once they are identified, once a light is shown upon them, they begin to diminish. Sometimes awareness alone will effectively eliminate negative effects of shadow traits. For instance, if I identify arrogance as a shadow trait, just knowing this on a conscious level may allow me to effectively manage the shadow's effect on me and my relationships.

In most cases, though, a lot more work is needed. The shadow trait just won't submit to control. With enough effort, we can sometimes, over a period of time, effectively diffuse these stubborn traits without help. Many of us, however, need some assistance in working through these issues. The need for help is not a sign of weakness and is nothing to be embarrassed about. Rather it is a sign of strength because we acknowledge and accept "what is." We are often quick to seek help from third parties in educating and training us, repairing our plumbing, mowing our lawn, treating our physical ailments, and teaching us a better golf stroke, but we somehow have been conditioned to think we are weak or unstable if we seek assistance with our emotional and behavior issues. It is ironic that if we really get the assistance we need with our emotional and behavioral issues, we would have fewer physical ailments, we would learn better, and we would operate with tremendous efficiency in all areas of our lives. We'd probably have better golf strokes too!

Actually, seeking help will put you on the leading edge of leadership training and development. *Business Week* recently reported a burgeoning trend in organizational management toward addressing leaders' childhood traumas and situations in an effort to reduce organizational dysfunction (Conlin 2004). Common childhood scenarios and their organizational reenactments include:

- The child's achievements were never enough and the leader today is a perfectionist, an approval seeker, and fears being a fraud.

- The parents inflated the child's importance and the leader today is overconfident, thinks he or she can do no wrong, and is above the rules.

- The child was forced to assume adult responsibilities too early and the leader today is overly responsible for others and is a workaholic.

- The child had a domineering parent and the leader today is fearful, freezing with bosses yet treating underlings as children.

- The child's problems and negative feelings were denied by the family and the leader today allows problems to fester to a crisis and expresses aggressiveness through sarcasm and humor.

The primary approach used by therapists today involves having the client experience repressed feelings over and over again until their destructive effects are largely diffused. The approach therapeutically shines the light, so to speak, on negative thoughts, emotions, and behaviors in the shadow. The client works to identify the events or conditions that caused them, reexperiencing those events or conditions repeatedly until the negative energy created by them is discharged. The client also works to learn how the event or conditions operate to affect his or her life today.

EXPOSING THE SHADOW TO THE LIGHT OF DAY

Shadow work focuses primarily on emotions, because they are the primary driver of behavior. *Emotions* can be understood as amplified thoughts you feel in your body. The initial test of what kind of emotion you are feeling is quite simple: are you happy or unhappy? If you feel happy, you are feeling things like bliss, excitement, empathy, compassion, joy, generosity, forgiveness, patience, tolerance, understanding, gentleness, respect, and honor. You should just be present and enjoy the emotion. Enjoy the love.

If you feel unhappy, then you have some work to do. The first thing to consider is that the emotion making you unhappy is a creation of your mind. The mind is separate from you. It does not want to be wrong.

Thus, the mind, as a matter of survival, will fight desperately to convince you that the emotion is justified. Remember, though, that the emotion is not real. It is a creation of the mind. It is born of fear. It thrives in the dark.

Unfortunately, emotions are usually such powerful bundles of energy that merely recognizing them for what they are—creations of the mind—is usually not enough to get rid of them. In fact, emotions that make you unhappy notify you that you have some buried emotional "land mines" that need to be discharged. Your mind cannot dismiss them because your body has already been engaged. You are already feeling them in your bones. You may be anxious. Your heart may race. You may get hot or chilled. You may shake. You may feel a pit in your stomach or feel your stomach sink. You can rationalize in your mind all day long about how a painful emotion has no logical justification, and it still will not go away. There is only one way to process the emotion successfully: feel it at your deepest level. Expose it to the light of the present moment. Anything else just denies the present moment.

EXERCISE:
EMOTIONAL MANAGEMENT

Beverly Engel, internationally known psychotherapist and best-selling author of a number of powerful self-help books, suggests the following exercise as an emotional management tool when a strong negative emotion arises in you (Engel 2005, 72–154):

STEP 1: IDENTIFY THE EMOTION

Are you feeling one of the primary emotions that make people unhappy—sorrow/sadness, anger, fear, or guilt/shame? Which one? Engel provides a masterful approach for accurately identifying the root emotion you are feeling. A key indicator is how your body feels. If you find yourself frowning, slumping, using a low, monotonous voice, feeling heaviness in your chest, feeling tired or empty, or wanting to cry or hide in bed, you are likely feeling sadness or sorrow. If you feel tightness, heat, an increase in heart rate or blood pressure, or your fists tightening, you are likely angry.

If you feel yourself perspiring, feeling nervous, jittery or jumpy, shaking, quivering or trembling, breathing fast, muscles tensing, a choking sensation, diarrhea, vomiting, feeling of heaviness in the stomach, or getting cold, you are likely experiencing fear. Guilt/shame, for a number of reasons explained by Engel, is often a difficult emotion to identify. Just as those who feel shame often want to hide from others, the emotion itself seems to want to hide. Some indicators include feeling a sense of dread, an intense desire to hide or cover your face, a pain in the pit of your stomach, blushing, nervousness, and nausea. Complicating matters more, those feelings of shame often jump right over the emotion and into sadness, anger, or fear.

STEP 2: IDENTIFY THE MESSAGE

Each emotion has a message for you. Sadness may be telling you that you experienced a loss or you had an expectation that was not met. Anger may be telling you that an important standard or rule in your life has been violated by someone else or yourself. It can also be telling you that your sadness has bubbled over into anger. Fear may be informing you that you are feeling powerless to handle a situation or need to prepare yourself to deal with a serious challenge. Guilt/shame may be saying that you violated your own standards.

STEP 3: FEEL THE EMOTION, BUT DON'T JUDGE

In what for me is the most difficult step, you experience the emotion without judging the emotion as bad. You just observe and feel. Practice, as well as the techniques and concepts discussed in chapter 1 on presence, will have you mastering this quickly.

STEP 4: ASK—IS IT APPROPRIATE TO BE FEELING THIS EMOTION?

Maybe your emotion in the present has been triggered by a past event. For instance, if my wife said within earshot of others at a social function,

"David, don't chew with your mouth open," I may feel anger toward her for embarrassing me. If my anger doesn't seem to dissipate, it is a signal to me that perhaps her comment made me feel something I felt as a young child. Perhaps it made me feel the same shame that I felt as a six-year-old when my father scolded me in front of others when he thought I was not being polite. I need to find a quiet space and feel that emotion that I felt as a child. Once my anger and shame over that childhood trauma dissipate, I find that my anger over my wife's comment is discharged. I might want to tell her gently in private that her comment hurt me and why it hurt me, and ask her to please try not to say such things at such times in the future. But anger has played no role in our interaction.

STEP 5: ACT TO REMEDY THE SITUATION

While you probably want to blame someone for your sadness, anger, fear, or shame, the reality is that you are responsible for your emotions and are better off asking how you need to change your perception of the situation. Are you overreacting? Are your expectations too high? Have you been triggered to feel a certain way by an event or condition that is minor in itself but acts as "salt in a wound"? Is the emotion appropriate right now? Do I need to communicate my needs and feelings? Do I need to behave differently in order to achieve different results?

I have used this exercise countless times, and found it very helpful in enhancing my own emotional, and ultimately behavioral, clarity. It shines a light on the element in my shadow that needs addressing in the moment. Without the light, that element works against me. It harms my relationships, hinders my decision making, and contributes to my discontent. With the light, I am more in control of my life, more secure, and less afraid. I have healthier relationships and make better choices.

This powerful exercise helps you to manage your shadow traits, to bring them out into the light and diffuse their power, so that they don't distort your thoughts, emotions, and behavior. With honest and sometimes painful work, you will be more self-defined and more people oriented. Also, more than ever before, you will also be able to build a values-based core and effectively engage your team. Simply put, people will understand you more, trust you more, like you more, and respect you more.

THE LEADER'S SHADOW

Parker J. Palmer, a writer, teacher, and activist, gave a speech in 1990 at the Annual Celebration Dinner of the Indiana Office for Campus Ministries entitled "Leading from Within: Reflections on Spirituality and Leadership." He described five typical shadows of a leader.

THE SHADOW OF DEEP INSECURITY. Bridget, head of a large human resources department, relies on titles, hierarchies, control, inaccessibility, and appearances to define her and her worth. Hard to spot in extraverted people, extraversion often exists in leaders precisely because they are insecure about themselves.

THE SHADOW OF HOSTILITY. Jerry, head of a national sales and marketing group, thinks the universe is hostile. Everything is a battle. Everything must be won, or he risks losing it all. The problem with this shadow is that it becomes a self-fulfilling prophecy. It creates an environment where people in Jerry's organization have to subscribe to that belief and act accordingly if they want to survive in the organization.

THE SHADOW OF FUNCTIONAL ATHEISM. This is a rather obscure title for a shadow, but it describes a leader who believes that everything —success, failure, day-to-day functions, major initiatives—depends upon him. "I know I act as if I believe in a higher being, but I don't really believe that. It is me who is responsible for everything."

THE SHADOW OF FEARING THE NATURAL CHAOS OF LIFE. The leader needs to control everything, even though nothing can truly be controlled.

THE SHADOW OF MORTALITY. John, head of a large bank's real estate lending group, doesn't understand that death is natural and it is out of death and decay that life and new creation emerge. So he protects what is still alive, as if allowing death is tantamount to failure. He stays with too many things—programs, objectives, strategies, tactics, methods—long after their useful lives.

SHINING THE LIGHT ON MY OWN SHADOW

I am not sure what ever happened to Ellen or Bill, described at the beginning of this chapter. I knew them, but have lost track of them. David, however, as I confessed earlier, is yours truly. Or he was me a number of years ago. At the time of my divorce, after a few years of meditating and becoming progressively more attuned to discontent deep within me, I had reached a point where I was ready to quit ignoring my pain and compensating for my fears. I reached a point where anything less than true contentment was insufficient, and I was ready to endure any transformational pain, for as long as necessary, to reach that objective.

I made a list of my negative emotions and behaviors that had become common in my life. Some were evident in my persona; others were securely hidden in my shadow. Some were pointed out by people very close to me, and others by people more distant. They included the following: shame about my basic nature; judging and being critical of others; self-criticism; workaholism; inability to be intimate in expressing my deepest feelings; lack of empathy for others; impatience; anger; trying to control others; and fear of abandonment.

I took my list—my long list—and called a therapist who had been recommended to me. I told him I needed his help in addressing these shadow traits. I began semiweekly sessions that lasted intermittently for years and changed my life for the better, dramatically and permanently. In subsequent years, I worked with several other outstanding therapists and, with their help, was able to cross a number of hurdles that finally have me living that life of contentment, peace, integrity, and love that had eluded me. As new issues—thoughts, emotions, and behaviors with which I am not comfortable or that cause problems in my relationships— arise, I go right back to counseling to work through the issues and regain clarity. I expect to do this for the rest of my life. Given how alive it makes me feel, and how beneficial it has been in my life, I look forward to it.

As illumination began to reveal my shadow and as I began to understand at the deepest level why my shadow traits exist and how they affect me, my leadership capabilities began to improve. The leadership characteristics that had been weakened by my fears became stronger—stronger than I could have imagined. My patience, openness, creativity, love for and sincere interest in people, as well as my courage and propensity to take risks, increased dramatically.

In retrospect, I noticed the biggest change in my self-definition. Prior to addressing my shadow issues and achieving a much higher degree of clarity, my ability to define myself—to know my values, beliefs, higher purpose, and vision of the future, and express them clearly—and to really engage with people was seriously compromised. People who worked on my teams at the time have since told me that I was an enigma: I preached the importance of a balanced life but was a workaholic and never home with my family. I would occasionally get angry at or be extremely critical of others. And I was extraordinarily impatient while stressing the importance of the long-term nature of what we were building. Some of them wondered whether I was really committed to the vision that I'd engaged them to pursue with me, or if I was more committed to making a lot of money for myself. Finally, some people sensed my uneasiness in communicating with them.

They were right. I was an enigma. I was an enigma to myself. I was too afraid to identify precisely that for which I stood, and then put a stake in the ground around that. Afraid of failure, of what people would think of me, and of what might be sacrificed by committing to anything and anyone, I always sought out the most acceptable and safest route or position instead of the one that most reflected my deepest beliefs and values.

In the several leadership positions I have held since developing my emotional and behavioral clarity, my ability to define myself has enhanced my ability to engage a team. I just care more about people than I ever did before. They sense it. They trust me more and are more willing to engage in the organizational effort I lead.

The High-Impact Leader Empowered by Clarity: Ramona

The high-impact leaders I have known were very fortunate in that they were raised in a highly positive, supportive environment that didn't encourage much of a shadow, were very resilient individuals who withstood the traumas of their youth with little damage, or had done some intense shadow work.

Ramona came to me several years ago when she was running a software company and trying to figure out what to do with it. I met with a number of her senior executives and employees to get a flavor for the organization and the industry it served. Her team thought she walked on water. They would follow her anywhere and do anything for her.

"It wasn't always that way," said Ramona. From the time she entered college, she wanted to work in a nonprofit organization serving the disadvantaged. After graduation, she joined an agency serving troubled inner-city youths. Within several years, she was running it. She was bright and extremely driven. Sixty- and seventy-hour workweeks were her norm.

Hours worked, though, were really just a part of her persona. It was a cover-up for a number of serious emotional and behavioral issues. She constantly feared failure. She could not express her feelings in a controlled way, rather she cried at the tiniest of provocations. If anyone merely questioned her judgment, she would break down. She was a merciless micromanager. At the end of the day, she believed, she would have to perform most tasks herself because no one else cared enough to do it as well as she could do it. She was painfully insecure about her appearance. She thought she was unattractive. She had become an emotional eater and was significantly overweight. Although she wanted an intimate relationship, she was unable to be intimate. She was depressed. A cloud of gloom always consumed her. To top it off, she drank too much and for the wrong reasons. She wouldn't call herself an alcoholic, but many would. When the occasion called for being sociable, she would drink to make herself feel comfortable in the setting. Occasionally, she would drink too much and feel hungover the next day. She always had a drink or two alone at night, "just to relax."

As a leader, she struggled with employee turnover. She blamed it on the nonprofit world. "I would always complain that I just couldn't pay enough to good people to hold on to them." For three years under her leadership, the organization's budget did not increase and its productivity—cases served—never increased. She was constantly struggling just to keep pace with the prior year's performance. She blamed the turnover, and her inability to pay more to employees, for the lack of progress.

Ramona resigned after three years of leading the agency. In her resignation letter, she said she had tired of carrying the full load of the organization and wanted to pursue other interests. In her youthful candor, she dished out some large portions of blame, thinly disguised as suggestions for future improvement.

She spent the next year looking for a job, exhausting her savings account, drinking more, and eating even more than that. In hindsight, she thinks she knew deep in her heart that she needed help and was intentionally sabotaging every opportunity for employment. She would show up late for the interview. Or she would condescend to the interviewer. Or she would be overly negative about her agency experience. Almost a year after leaving the agency, she was diagnosed as a diabetic. For Ramona, this was her "bottom." A doctor was telling her that her two primary crutches in life—high carbohydrate foods and alcohol—were off limits. She fell and fell hard. Of her own accord, she called a counselor that she used to employ at the agency and the counselor agreed to work with her on a deferred payment plan.

Fortunately, the counselor was very good. Ramona trusted him, probably more out of desperation than anything else. But her trust allowed the counselor to work very quickly with her to get at the crux of her problems. Ramona's mother had abused her terribly. She would hit her frequently, often raising welts on her cheeks and head. She criticized her constantly, often telling her that no man would ever be attracted to her with her ugly appearance and lack of intelligence and grace. Her father was emotionally unavailable throughout her childhood. He worked two jobs and was rarely home. When he was home, he was glued to the television.

Ramona emerged as an adult with a great amount of fear, anger, shame, and sadness. They were all tucked away in her shadow while her workaholic persona kept busy with the practical vicissitudes of life. She feared everyone would reject her as her mother had. She feared failing and making all her mother's predictions true. She was mad at her mother for the obvious reasons. She was mad at her father for effectively abandoning her. She felt an immense amount of shame about being who she was. Everything she did to disguise her shame—overeating, drinking, being critical of others—only caused her to feel more shame. She was sad that she didn't have supportive parents. She was sad that she didn't feel loved and protected as a child.

Once Ramona started talking openly about her feelings— exposing the shadow to the healing light of day—she started to feel lighter, figuratively and physically. Once she felt those things buried in her shadow, really felt them, they didn't seem so heavy. Their energy, and hence its power over her, was slowly discharged. Within several weeks, she was actually feeling episodes of joy. Within several months, joy had become her natural state. She also started feeling lighter in the literal sense. She lost weight. She stopped drinking, began engaging with people on an intimate level, and started getting called back for second interviews.

Ramona finally got a job as a business development officer with a small software company. That job led to a position with another company as head of sales and marketing. She initially joined her current company in the same role, but was promoted to chief executive officer after several years. My discussions with her team members revealed a Ramona who could not have been more different from the way Ramona described herself as being years before.

This Ramona was extraordinarily self-defined. She knew precisely who she was, what she believed in, and where she was going. Her words and actions conveyed the same, in a consistent manner, to her team members. She was authentically people oriented. She wasn't a glad-hander and didn't chat for the sake of chatting. She cared about a real exchange of thoughts, feelings, ideas, and values with other people. She trusted people and their ability to work for the benefit of the organizational objective. She had learned to delegate. She had read the classic work by James Collins and Jerry Porras (1994, 48), *Built to Last*, and knew the importance of a *core ideology*, or core values combined with a fundamental purpose for existing beyond just making money, to a company's success. She embodied a higher purpose—openness and creativity in the pursuit of organizational efficiency—that attracted and engaged team members to want to work with her in developing software products that improved the flow of life.

Under her leadership, the company's revenues had increased tenfold, and profits had increased thirtyfold. From a strategic standpoint, her company had a lot of options open to it. I could help her explore them. This would be the easy part. She had already done all the heavy lifting, unloading the long bag behind her.

THE LEADERSHIP DASHBOARD

Figure 3.1, the Leadership Dashboard, shows the extent to which clarity of thought, emotion, and behavior enhances a leader's ability to embody key character traits and perform critical leadership functions described in the introduction. It shows that built upon the foundation of presence, which allows you to begin to identify negative characteristics that undermine your relationships, desire for contentment, and ability to lead in the most effective way possible, clarity is a powerful driver enabling you to:

BE SELF-DEFINED. People will not follow you unless they know and respect who you are, what you believe, what you value, and where you are going. Clarity allows you to intimately know these things and express them clearly.

BE PEOPLE-ORIENTED. You may be people-oriented in that extra-verted, superficial way that leaders often are, but you won't be authentically people-oriented—truly intimate with and interested in loving other people—until you have come to understand and love yourself. Once you do, and you no longer feel shame about what lurks in your shadow, you become openhearted, with a genuine love for people.

BUILD A VALUES-BASED CORE. Feeling secure enough to know that there is only one master in your life whom you must please, you are able to translate your self-definition into your organization's ability to say, in the words of James Collins and Jerry Porras (1994, 54), "[T]his is who we are; this is what we stand for; this is what we are all about."

ENGAGE A TEAM. As a leader, you must engage the hearts of your team members before their minds and bodies will follow. The only way to engage their hearts is to engage your own. The only way to engage your own is to know yourself and your shadow thoroughly.

Clarity of thought, emotion, and behavior also facilitates your ability to:

BE FORWARD THINKING. Liberated from fear, you will be open to the possibilities of the future.

BE CREDIBLE. Lack of clarity in thought, emotion, and behavior usually means there is a "long bag" behind you. In other words, there is a great disparity between who you are representing yourself to be—your persona—and who you really are. People sense the inconsistency and your credibility is diminished. With clarity comes genuineness. It enables you to display consistency and wholeness in your words and behavior, such that others have a deep confidence in your abilities and character.

BE INSPIRING. With your mind uncluttered by fear-based thoughts, emotions, and behavior, you are able to listen deeply to your team members to discover a common purpose, then give life to your vision by communicating it so that they see themselves in it.

BE ENERGETIC. The lack of clarity of thought, emotion, and behavior, and the presence of fears underlying them, is draining. Clarity frees your energy for use in positive ways as you lead your organization.

BE CURIOUS. People with big shadows deal with a great degree of fear. People who are fearful tend to avoid the new and unknown. Becoming less afraid stimulates your inquisitive sense and eagerness to learn.

BE FOCUSED. Just as lack of clarity drains energy, lack of clarity also interferes with your ability to focus with the laserlike precision needed in our high velocity, highly complex existence. Clarity enables you to concentrate your energy and attention in the pursuit of your objective.

BE COURAGEOUS. Lessen your fear-based shadow traits, and you'll find yourself more able than ever to make the tough calls, perform the tough tasks, and take risks that differentiate you from the ordinary leader.

BE ORGANIZED. Clear thinking and emoting leads to clear behavior. Your ability to coordinate and direct activities in a functional, structured whole will be better than ever.

BE SUPPORTIVE. Clarity empowers you with the sense of security. This allows you to dedicate yourself to strengthening others by fostering an environment that encourages risk taking, collaboration, self-leadership, and recognition.

GENERATE IDEAS. Secure with yourself and unafraid of being a pioneer, you will be a thought leader, identifying new associations and connections, and originating new or alternative concepts, approaches, processes, and objectives.

FORM A VISION. Thinking and emoting more clearly, you will process ideas and possibilities into an organizational objective with ease.

CREATE ACCOUNTABILITY. Clarity will allow you to lead with a fine balance of collaboration, which encourages each individual to contribute his or her share, and firmness, which requires each individual to contribute his or her share.

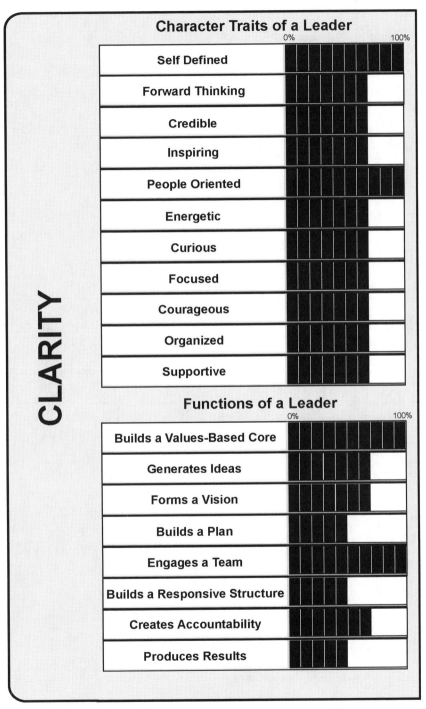

FIGURE 3.1

CHAPTER 4

INTENTION

The Fourth Driver of the High-Impact Leader

Intention, or more accurately practiced intention, is a powerful transformational driver that exists within each of us. This chapter will show how to maximize the power of practiced intention within yourself and, as a leader, use it as fuel to be focused and organized, build a plan, and produce results.

INTENTION: THE SEED OF POSSIBILITY

An *intention* is a desire for a result. We all have intentions, many of them. But we may not be getting the results we desire.

Intentions alone have little meaningful effect, and it doesn't help when we readily abandon them in favor of new ones. For example, perhaps you yearn for some extended downtime one minute, and then you take on a huge, time-consuming project the next.

> **An *intention* is a desire for a result.**

When you feel and then express an intention for a result, you give yourself a more-than-random chance of achieving the result. But it is only a slightly more-than-random chance. It is a seed of possibility. But like a seed, it doesn't grow without being nurtured.

Intention to act in a certain way or bring about a certain result can be powerful. But to have any meaningful effect, intention needs to be embodied in practice. In the same way that you can only be truly kind and generous if you practice kindness and generosity, you will not achieve your desired results if you don't practice your intention.

PRACTICED INTENTION: THE RIPENING OF PROBABILITY

Dr. Masaru Emoto is a highly creative and visionary Japanese researcher, and author of several books, including *The True Power of Water* (2005). His work strongly suggests that our thoughts affect everything in and around us. Specifically, Dr. Emoto demonstrates this by photographs of tap water taken before and after people directed positive or negative intentions to it. Water that received thoughts of love or gratitude morphed into beautiful crystalline structures. Water that received negative thoughts morphed into very ugly structures and appearances. The water was exposed to many other energetic influences, such as different types of music, other sounds, words, ideas, and images, and the same kind of results occurred. Love and gratitude produced structures of beauty, and negativity produced ugliness.

Whatever you think of Dr. Emoto's research, and there is certainly room for debate, I believe it is evidence that you can use intention to change the conditions in your life and the course of events. Consider that water comprises over 70 percent of a human body and covers the same amount of our planet. Water is the very source of all life on this planet. Dr. Emoto's work suggests to me that we can influence that core element with our thoughts alone. If we can change the molecular structure of water, we can change the molecular structure of ourselves. We can change the molecular structure of others. We can change the molecular structure of matter, which is only crystallized energy. And we can change the conditions in our lives and the course of events. We just have to believe we can and we have to practice.

THE PRINCETON STUDIES ON INTENTION

In studies that began in 1979 at Princeton University's Engineering Anomalies Research (PEAR) lab, extraordinary results were produced in a number of experiments over many years that strongly support the power of intention. This fascinating program, focused on evaluating the effect of human consciousness on machines, utilized a number of different machines carefully calibrated to generate random results. One machine, for instance, contained thousands of balls that, when the machine was turned upside down, would bounce off randomly placed pegs and ultimately fall into one of nineteen compartments. Another was a computer that spit out random numerals. Another was a small robot that swiveled around randomly on a small table. Each machine, without any human influence, produced completely random results.

The scientists, however, found that the intention of volunteers influenced the results produced by these machines at a statistically significant level (Dunne and Jahn 1992). The specific findings are compelling. First, they found the period of time between the expression of the intention and generation of results did not matter. When volunteers focused their intentions on a result, that intention could precede the running of the program by days. Astoundingly, the researchers also found that an intention expressed after the fact—after the machine had generated results—influenced the results to a statistically significant level. Second, they found that distance between the person or persons expressing the intention and the machine generating the results did not matter. A volunteer on the other side of the world could focus his or her intention on a machine and that intention would produce the same result as if he or she were draped over it.

> In the same way that you can only be truly kind and generous if you practice kindness and generosity, you will not achieve your desired results if you don't practice your intention.

Some other results are equally fascinating. The studies showed that pairs of people had a greater impact on results than a single person (Dunne 1991). They also found that two people in love have six times the effect of a single person!

THE FINDINGS OF NAPOLEON HILL: INTENTION AND SUCCESS

I am still amazed by the number of people who have never heard of a phenomenal book first published in 1937 entitled *Think and Grow Rich* (Hill 1960). The author, Napoleon Hill, was commissioned by the famous and wealthy industrialist Andrew Carnegie in the early twentieth century to interview hundreds of the world's most successful people in an effort to learn the secret of their success. Hill spent decades interviewing the likes of Henry Ford, William Wrigley Jr., George Eastman, Wilbur Wright, John D. Rockefeller, Thomas A. Edison, Clarence Darrow, Luther Burbank, and Alexander Graham Bell. He found that practiced intention was the single-most important determinant of personal and professional success.

WHY WE DON'T PRACTICE INTENTION

If intention is so powerful, why aren't we doing a better job of using it to our advantage?

WE LACK FAITH. Most of us simply do not believe that we can attain our desired results, and that we can change the conditions and the course of events in our lives. For instance, almost everyone I have met has a desire to do something different in his or her life. A corporate executive wants to start a nonprofit. A plumber wants to be a corporate executive. A short-order cook wants to become a renowned chef. But they just sit there passively with this intention, wondering if it might become a reality someday. While most people constantly say or think "I hope" and "I want" and "I'd like," few of us sincerely believe we can bring about a desired result. Thus, we leave our fates to the four winds or, perhaps worse, to the intentions of others.

WE NEGLECT OUR POWER. Most of us are too busy, distracted, stressed, unfocused, and ungrounded. We are too mired in the past or future. For example, suppose I have an intention of building my company to a size that would merit a sale for $10 million. But each day I neglect my power to make that happen by doing everything but the things that will make it happen. I launch too many unrelated product lines out of fear that one line will fail and I'll need other lines to make up for the failure. I spend time micromanaging my team members in daily activities because I don't trust that they can do them successfully on their own. I saddle the company with too much debt because it's easier than tightly managing my cash flow.

WE FEAR OUR POWER. For reasons that support the entire practice of psychotherapy, many of us don't want the power to attain our desired results. We don't trust ourselves with the power. We think we will ultimately fail even if we are successful in realizing the immediate intention. We don't want to go any higher or attain any more because we would have further to fall and more to lose.

EXERCISE:
THE GROWTH OF PROBABILITY

The practice of intention involves investing energy into achieving a desired result. It requires complete awareness of the forces conspiring for and against the desired result. It requires opening a dialogue with possibility about your desired result. It requires ritual and focus. Finally, it requires faith that life will deliver the best result to you.

This exercise is one of practiced intention. It will generate powerful energy behind and around your intentions. It will transform your possibilities into probabilities. As a leader, you will start to experience an enhanced ability to focus, to concentrate your energy and attention in the pursuit of your objective. You will be more capable of organizing, of coordinating and directing activities in a functional, structured whole.

You will be more capable than ever of building a plan that defines the optimal path from your vision to your objectives. Finally, you will achieve your organizational vision in the most efficient, holistic, and measurable manner possible.

STEP 1: BE PRESENT

Presence, being conscious and mindful of all around you (see chapter 1), enables you to be more certain that the desired result is truly the best result and what you want. It allows you to better define your intention. It brings into view the forces working in favor of the desired result and the forces working against it.

STEP 2: EXPRESS YOUR INTENTION IN DETAIL

Define very clearly and with great specificity your intention. In formulating your intention, use the present tense, as if what you want is already happening. The present moment is all there is and all you have. Having an intention means that, at some future moment, you want that moment to have certain qualities. Describe those qualities as if you are in the future moment, enjoying your intentions come true. Thus, instead of laying out your intention as a plan for what the future will look like, describe it as a present condition.

Specify the precise time that you are targeting. Specify a plan. Consider how your intention will be realized. This alone is a huge step for most people. If I want to sell my company for $10 million, I might start out defining my intention in no more detailed terms than this: "I want to sell my company for $10 million."

However, what I should be saying, if I want to build energy around my intention, is this: "It is December 31, 2008. I am selling my company for $10 million in cash. My company generates annual revenue of $10 million and cash flow of $2 million. This revenue is generated 40 percent from sales of Product A, 30 percent from Product B, and 30 percent from Product C. Our cost of goods sold is 50 percent. We sell nationally and internationally, with international sales constituting 10 percent of our revenue. We have no more than $1 million in debt at the time of sale."

Journaling can help you make your intention concrete. Buy a blank journal and write out everything you intend, in all the detail you can. I encourage clients to write a short story, documentary, or docudrama, filling it with specifics, even to the point of extreme. I might conclude my writing about my intention with something like this: "It is December 31, 2008. I am at my lawyer's office for our closing. I am wearing jeans and a T-shirt. My bag is packed for a monthlong trip to Bali. As I sign the closing papers, the money is being wired to my account at Bank of America. Of that money, $500,000 goes to pay off my home mortgage. The local BMW dealership receives $75,000 for full payment on a new 550i. Another $75,000 goes to the local nonprofit providing home meals for senior citizens. I feel complete and satisfied."

When you are leading an organization, you must have a plan. After two decades of working with leaders, I am still astounded by the number of leaders who try to operate without a plan. They say, "I know I should, but I have been too busy," or "My plan is in my head." It is crucial to have a well-conceived, well-articulated plan that is transparent to everyone in the organization. Otherwise, you do a disservice to everyone else in the organization. They spend a large part of their lives trying to find purpose in their own lives and organizational roles, and trying to achieve what they believe are organizational objectives. They deserve to know the plan. Likewise, you deserve to know the plan that will bring your intention to fruition.

Once written, continue to rewrite your intention, as often as you can, even if it doesn't change from writing to writing. Read the plan aloud when you wake up in the morning and before you go to bed at night. If you can find other times to read it, do so—the more, the better. As you read it, try to feel the plan as a reality.

STEP 3: VISUALIZE IT

One of the most powerful steps in the practice of intention is to go deep inside yourself and see your intention playing out in your mind and body. For the past thirty years or so, top-caliber athletes like Joe Montana, arguably the best quarterback in the history of pro football, and Brian Boitano, a 1988 Olympic gold medal–winner in skating, have been using visualization, or guided imagery, as a means of optimizing their performance (Montana and Mitchell 2005, 131–40). They imagine very detailed scenarios, down to the sound of the crowd, and the feel of the air on their skin, and visualize their desired performance. They play these images over and over again. With each repetition, the likelihood of actually performing as visualized increases. Guided imagery is being used increasingly in all walks of life. Montana, for instance, continues to use it in his business career. And many people have told me that they are successfully using it, at the direction of their doctors and other healers, in treating a number of physical and mental ailments. Although there are a number of different techniques, I suggest the following:

PREPARE FOR VISUALIZATION

I suggest allocating twenty or thirty minutes of time in which you will not be disturbed. Find a quiet, comfortable space. Avoid the bed because it is too easy to fall asleep. Rather, sit on a chair, meditation bench, or cushion on the floor. Sit erect and try not to lean backward against the seat back; slumping backward against a rest tends to induce sleep. Just as in meditation, an erect posture with chin slightly tucked is ideal.

If you are in a chair, place your bare feet firmly on the floor. If on a meditation cushion or bench, cross your legs or tuck them under or beside you (toes pointing behind you), again keeping your spine erect. There are many different hand positions. Try different ones until you find one that works for you. (For guided imagery, I usually open my hands and face my palms upward.) Then close your eyes.

BEGIN RELAXATION

Close your mouth and start to breathe through your nose. As you draw in your breath, fully experience it. Feel the coolness of the air as it passes through your nostrils and starts to fill your lungs. Feel your chest expand with oxygen. Feel its essential nature—it is your lifeblood. As you exhale, feel your chest contract. Feel the warmth of your breath as it passes through your nostrils.

After two or three minutes of this, begin a progressive relaxation.

RELAX PROGRESSIVELY

Focus your attention on your toes and feel them relax completely. When they feel relaxed, focus on the ball of your foot. When that is relaxed, move to your instep, and so on up your legs and body until your entire body is completely relaxed. Sometimes this progressive relaxation may take awhile in the learning stages, but with experience comes speed. Soon you'll be relaxed in two or three minutes.

PICTURE A PEACEFUL, PLEASANT SCENE

Now picture yourself in the most pleasant scene you can conjure up in your mind. Something peaceful, serene, safe, and beautiful—perhaps you're on a bluff overlooking the ocean on a beautiful day, or you're in a peaceful meadow surrounded by lush trees.

IMAGINE A SCREEN IN FRONT OF YOU

Once you feel immersed in your setting, imagine a large screen in front of you. It is surrounded by a brilliant gold frame.

CREATE YOUR INTENTION ON THE SCREEN

Start to "show" your intention on the screen, as if you were viewing a movie. There are no limits. Create your intended scenario with as much detail as you can provide. Surround your scene with soft light, representative of all colors of the spectrum (and hence infinite possibilities) as well as purity, joy, and spiritual power. Then play the scenario over in your mind a couple times, again with all the detail you can provide. Do this every day, twice a day if you can.

STEP 4: OFFER EXCHANGE

We all know the rule: nothing in life is free. Nothing comes without an exchange. Be clear on what you will exchange for your intention. If

I were focused on selling my company, I might say, "I have reduced my annual salary from $250,000 to $75,000 to increase cash flow. I increased my weekly time commitment to the company from forty-five hours to sixty hours. I am granting each of my three top executives an option to purchase 3 percent of the company so that they are completely motivated to achieve my objectives."

STEP 5: START A CONSPIRACY

Recruit people to make your intended result a reality. The intentions of many have an exponentially greater effect than the intentions of one. Of particular importance are the people you love. Enlist your spouse or partner, your children and friends, and your team members in your organization. It can be as easy as just talking about your intention. Most will feel your energy and, if they care at all about you, will start to echo your intention. It may well evolve, if it's appropriate, into a full-blown conspiracy involving investors, team members, professional service providers, and vendors.

STEP 6: EXPRESS GRATITUDE

Gratitude is a powerful expression of intention. When you send the energy of appreciation out into the world, I believe the likelihood of your intentions becoming reality is dramatically increased. I believe that when the collective energies outside of us—other people, other forms of life, our physical environment, higher powers—feel the energy of our appreciation, they react just like we do when someone expresses appreciation to us: they want even more to please us.

Also, expressing gratitude—relating not necessarily to your intention, but to anything for which you are thankful—is a wonderful, transformative habit. Feel it. Journal it. Think it. Verbally express it. As I discussed in chapter 1, one of the great things about the expression of gratitude is that it requires being in the present moment. Sincere gratitude cannot be expressed while not in the present.

STEP 7: LET IT GO

If you practice intention, will your intentions become reality? Some will, but certainly not all of them. Why not? Because there is a larger picture we cannot see. We believe some intentions are best for us, but they really aren't, for reasons that are hidden to us. How many times have you wished for something that would come true for you, and years later said, "I'm so thankful that did not come true"? I can remember certain jobs I wanted in the worst way, and I prayed so hard that I would get them. Several years after not getting them, I was able to see that they were not best for me: some other career opportunity unfolded that dwarfed the one on which I was so focused or something else happened that was much better for me.

Some ask, "Why have or practice any intention if you don't know if it will come to be?" My answer is that you have the first word. Your input—your intentions—are powerful factors in determining what will happen. To not practice intention is to subject yourself to completely random results. And I don't believe we were given free will so that we could ignore it in favor of randomness.

So the best thing you can do as a concluding step in your practice of intention is to detach from your intended result. You've done all you can. Now trust that what is best will happen. And it will.

"POSTGRADUATE" WORK IN PRACTICED INTENTION

The kind of practiced intention I have discussed—that which is directed toward a specific desired result—is powerful, and often astoundingly so. Veterans of practiced intention, though, will tell you that there is an even more powerful practice of intention that is directed toward achieving a nonspecific, general result. In fact, Sophy Burnham (2002, 63–67), the author of *The Path of Prayer*, has abandoned prayer for a specific result in favor of prayer for a general result. Burnham suggests that the universe, which has the last word on results, appreciates the power of a general expression more than the force of a specific intention because the first has more respect for its divine wisdom than the latter.

Thus, if I had an intention of selling my business in 2008, I might supplement my practiced intention for specific results, or even replace it, with practiced intention for general results. I might instead ask for more free time—and the resources to finance it—to devote to my family and friends, travel, expanding my spiritual practice, and giving back to the community. I might be given all this in a way that is even more generous than I envisioned. For instance, perhaps the sales of my products catch fire and quadruple in the next couple of years. I take my company public at a $100 million valuation. My new board of directors decides to hire a new chief executive. They pay me a severance of $3 million and sign me to a ten-year consulting contract of $250,000 annually. The work required of me is minimal. Several years later, a much larger competitor buys the company for $500 million and I am paid $125 million for my stake.

The high-impact leader within you recognizes that desire alone is not enough. It has to be ignited by an active practice. You wake up every morning and describe in writing and aloud, with great specificity, your intentions. You review the writings throughout the day and before going to sleep at night. You meditate on it and pray for it. These affirmations begin to cause an energetic shift in you and in your environment. You start to notice doors opening and start exploring what lies beyond. Conditions start aligning with your intentions and those intentions start shaping reality. Your desires are fulfilled while the great majority of leaders quietly wish away in their minds—and all because you believed in the power of your intention. Believe you have this power, and you'll have it. Don't believe it, and you won't.

The High-Impact Leader Empowered by Intention: Suzanne

Suzanne was elected chairperson of a committee interested in building a new private school in her community. She had worked with the group for almost three years, and was elected to the chair after her three predecessors quit in frustration. Although the group shared a general interest in building a new academically oriented school that would offer a clear alternative to public school, it disagreed on just about everything else. No matter how hard it tried, or what it tried, it could not gain traction in any one direction. In a group of twenty-eight people, there seemed to be twenty-eight factions and twenty-eight agendas: One person wanted a world-class athletic program. Another a world-class music program. Another a world-class student exchange program. One person wanted uniforms and strict discipline. Another wanted minimal rules and maximum freedom for the students to encourage their creativity. One person wanted to rent an old warehouse and convert it to their purpose, and another wanted to raise $25 million in a capital campaign to build a gleaming new structure. One person wanted a headmaster from an elite private school in New England, and another wanted a principal from a local school who had expressed an interest.

Each monthly meeting went on for hours and accomplished nothing. People would quit the board and others would join. Suzanne wondered to herself many times why she remained involved. She just kept thinking that something would happen to galvanize the group and give it traction.

She was elected chairperson on a night when her immediate predecessor raged at the whole group and stormed out, leaving behind a trail of four-letter words and a lot of ill will. The group turned to her because she was its longest-standing member and was well liked. When she got home that night, she cried. She was already busy enough with her job as a marketing consultant and raising children with her partner, Elizabeth. This was the last thing she needed. As she and Elizabeth talked, however, she remembered again her purpose for getting involved in the first place: she wanted to create a school where their children and others in the community could truly thrive. She had to give it one last effort.

This was Suzanne's first real leadership opportunity. She had been a successful student, athlete, and sales professional at a major consumer products company, but had never led a group of people. She had read a number of leadership books, though, and was steeped in the character traits of a successful leader and the functions that a leader would perform. Nevertheless, as she sat

111

talking with Elizabeth, she felt overwhelmed by this leadership task. How would she ever break the group's inertia?

Elizabeth reminded her of their practices of intention they had used while attempting to adopt their children years before. All of a sudden, it hit Suzanne that the same practices could be used here, and anywhere, for that matter. Amidst the stresses of everyday life, she had strayed from them in recent years. But now was the time to reengage.

She resumed her meditation practice to ensure she was as grounded as she could be. She spent all of her free time over the next week writing a detailed plan for success. After so much time invested in the project, she had all the data she needed to accurately describe, in great detail, the market opportunity, and what she perceived to be the best vision for the school as well as the best operating plan for success. She journaled an offer of exchange to herself. Specifically, she committed to herself in her journal to devote four nights a week to the project, understanding that it would reduce her family and recreational time as well as her income.

She then began meeting with the people she believed were the opinion leaders of the large group. She gave them her written plan and described in detail what success would look like. She found they respected the fact that she was investing a lot of energy in creating traction. Most of them became less contentious and tabled their own agendas in favor of Suzanne's. They seemed to realize that they could each have their personal visions and no school, or a collective vision and a school.

Beyond the working group, Suzanne began wearing the project on her sleeve. She started a conspiracy. She started telling everyone she knew that she was heading up a group building a new school that would open within eighteen months. And every night, she would take twenty minutes before going to sleep to visualize every element of the new school she could imagine. And then she would spend a few minutes letting go of her specific desired result, thanking the universe for all of the good things in her life and expressing trust that perfection would result.

112

Eighteen months later, the group, under Suzanne's leadership, opened a new school in a temporary facility with plans for a permanent facility. Her practice of intention was a critical personal driver that enabled her to be focused and organized, build a plan, and ultimately achieve a successful result. She likened it to a laser beam cutting through scar tissue. It cut through all the egos, conflict, and fatigue that had paralyzed the group prior to her leadership.

THE LEADERSHIP DASHBOARD

The Leadership Dashboard (figure 4.1) graphically shows the effect of practiced intention on a leader's ability to embody the key character traits and perform the critical leadership functions described in the introduction. On a 100-point scale, it shows the powerful driver of intention, built upon a foundation of presence that allows you to create and clearly define your best intentions. It also shows how intention helps you identify and manage the factors working to make the desired result a reality as well as those working against it. This powerful fuel enables you to:

BE FOCUSED. Practiced intention concentrates your energy and attention in the pursuit of your personal and organizational objectives.

BE ORGANIZED. The awareness, as well as energetic force, of practiced intention enables you to coordinate and direct activities necessary to achieve your objectives in a functional, structured whole.

BUILD A PLAN. Intention requires that you create and define the optimal path connecting vision to results.

PRODUCE RESULTS. As Napoleon Hill (1960) found, intention is the single-most important factor in achieving your personal and organizational objectives.

To a lesser extent, but still in a powerful way, the energy of intention will also fuel your ability to:

BE SELF-DEFINED. The practice of intention requires that you know your values, beliefs, higher purpose, and vision of the future, and that you express them clearly.

BE FORWARD THINKING. Intention compels you to envision an extraordinary, exciting, and ennobling future.

BE CREDIBLE. Practiced intention makes you much more able to display consistency and wholeness in your words and behavior, such that others have a deep confidence in your commitment to the organizational purpose.

BE INSPIRING. Intention, practiced at its best, results in your giving life to your vision in a way that your team members see themselves in it.

BE PEOPLE-ORIENTED. The grounding required in practiced intention allows you to see the value in lives around you and your connection to them.

BE ENERGETIC. Although a lot of energy goes into the practice of intention, it all comes back to you and your organization.

ENGAGE A TEAM. Intention is the energetic infrastructure enabling you to recruit, engage, and inspire people to execute the realization of the vision.

BUILD A RESPONSIVE STRUCTURE. Intention requires you to structure your organization such that it is optimally suited to achieve your objective—that is, a permeable organization that is highly adaptive and responsive to changing conditions in the dynamic, high velocity, highly complex, interconnected world in which your organization exists.

CREATE ACCOUNTABILITY. Practiced intention by you as a leader effectively demands that your team members contribute their share toward accomplishing the organizational vision.

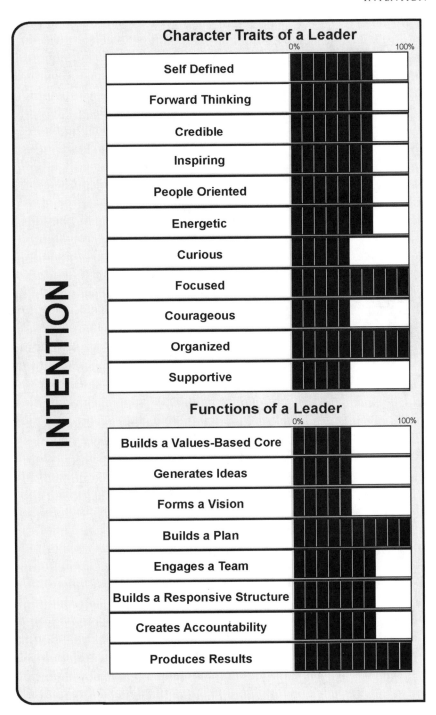

FIGURE 4.1

CHAPTER 5

PERSONAL RESPONSIBILITY

The Fifth Driver of the High-Impact Leader

Chapter 2 addressed openness, which is the willingness to consider every element of "what is." This chapter addresses *personal responsibility*, the complete personal ownership of "what is." Why should you take personal responsibility for everything that happens? Surely not everything that goes wrong is your fault, so why take the responsibility? This view of the world presumes that taking responsibility will have only negative consequences.

In this chapter, I'll show how taking responsibility—even for things that aren't your fault—can give you tremendous power. I'll explore how our culture has strayed so far from personal responsibility in the past couple of generations, and I'll show you how to reclaim it. Finally, I'll demonstrate how personal responsibility is the essential fuel for a leader's ability to be credible and courageous, as well as to build a plan and create accountability.

THE CULTURE OF BLAME AND DISOWNMENT

A person with a bad heart and high blood pressure may blame it on fast-food purveyors who serve large-sized servings laced with all the fat, trans-fatty acids, sugars, and chemicals that made the food appealing in the first place. That person then sues them and recovers money when he suffers a heart attack or stroke. A person who develops lung cancer after smoking for forty years sues a tobacco company for selling the cigarettes. A person invests in a company's stock, then sues the company when the stock price falls. A person who received medical treatment that didn't work sues the doctor and the hospital for negligence, the pharmaceutical company for product liability, and the insurance company for bad-faith handling of the insurance claim. I'm sure you can think of many more examples of how we avoid taking responsibility for our own actions and then blame others for the consequences.

Whatever the situation, it's tempting to avoid taking personal responsibility. There is no readily apparent benefit in it. If we say, "This event or condition is my sole responsibility," we will likely get sued, fired, demoted, criticized, imprisoned, or dropped by our insurance company. This is our culture, a culture of blame. And we are a population of victims.

Where there isn't anyone to blame, it's easy to deny or disown "what is." We may say, "It isn't my fault," "It isn't my responsibility," "I am not responsible for my ill health," "I am not responsible for global warming," "I am not responsible for the sorry state of the streets in my city." Sound familiar?

Even when we don't avoid personal responsibility by blaming or disowning, we may neglect "what is," including the fact we have personal responsibility. We know about global warming, but we show our neglect by ignoring it. We know eating unhealthy foods may kill us, but we ignore that fact. We know we are unhappy, but we may not give it much thought.

When we avoid taking responsibility, we pass up the opportunity to make a difference in the situation. If we don't participate in the solution, we contribute to the problem. We end up feeling that we are

> By taking responsibility, you become part of the solution. As a leader, this is your role.

completely at the mercy of people and forces over which we have no control. We lack power. And yet, taking responsibility gives us—gives you—power. By taking responsibility, you become part of the solution. As a leader, this is your role.

HOW WE GOT HERE

Who really knows how our culture shifted so far from personal responsibility? The chicken-and-egg conundrum is hard at work. It is difficult to identify cause and effect. For instance, did lawyers cause the proliferation of tort litigation? Or did citizens cause it by electing representatives who favored the shifting of responsibility? Here are some of the things I believe have conspired to contribute to the current culture:

OUR SENSE OF COMMUNITY HAS ERODED

Through technology and our corresponding high standard of living, most of us have lost touch with the sources of production. In centuries past, we collaborated to produce many of the necessities in life, or we were very close to most of the sources. Perhaps our neighbor raised the eggs with which we fed our family, and our brother worked at the local power plant that produced our electricity, and our sister worked at the textile plant that produced the fabric for our clothes.

Today we are separate from almost everything. Our power comes from a plant owned by a big public company five hundred miles away. Our clothes come from overseas. Our food is distributed by multinational corporations. Community plays a much diminished role in our lives. This has resulted in a loss of connection with the world around us and a lack of empathy for others. Years ago, we wouldn't have sued our egg-producing neighbor for salmonella poisoning because we knew him and liked him and understood his plight. Today many of us would file a multimillion dollar lawsuit against the egg producer, the grocery store chain, and perhaps the government for inadequate regulation.

LITIGATION BECAME A TOOL FOR CHANGE

Walter Olson (1991), senior fellow at the Manhattan Institute Center for Legal Policy, describes how, up until about thirty years ago, litigation was considered an act of last resort—a necessary evil, if you will. Ethical rules discouraged lawyers from "stirring up" lawsuits, and procedural rules put the expense of litigation largely on the plaintiff. Rules of evidence discouraged claims that lacked solid factual support at the outset.

In the past three decades, however, filing a lawsuit has insidiously shifted from the last thing you would do to exact some compensation for a harm you suffered to a powerful tool to effect social change. Nowadays, if we want Detroit to make safer cars, we allow some injured plaintiffs to sue auto manufacturers and recover hundreds of millions of dollars. If we want to stop people from smoking, we allow some lung-cancer patients to sue the tobacco companies. Once litigation was considered a good thing for society, courts and legislators opened the floodgates. In 1977, the U.S. Supreme Court, in *Bates v. State Bar of Arizona*, decided that lawyers have the constitutional right to advertise. Now advertisements encourage people to file lawsuits. Civil procedure rules were revamped to make it easier to sue and harder to get a lawsuit dismissed. The rewards for suing—monetary damages—increased dramatically. Punitive damages became commonplace, as did contingency fees for lawyers. It became easier to file class-action lawsuits.

RIGHTS DWARF RESPONSIBILITY

Over many generations, at least here in the United States, courts and legislatures have greatly expanded their recognition of a citizen's rights. While this is undoubtedly a good thing, there has not been a similar focus on a citizen's responsibilities. Hence, we have become preoccupied with our rights at the expense of attention to our personal responsibilities.

SIZE AND COMPLEXITY OF OUR EXISTENCE

With over six billion people on the planet, many of whom live increasingly fast-paced and complex lives, it's easy to see how individual involvement in any facet of life beyond our day-to-day activities, from government to social and environmental causes, can seem insignificant. If you feel like you are at the mercy of the world instead of having an effect on it, you may not be too inspired to take responsibility for your current condition.

THE VITAL IMPORTANCE OF TAKING RESPONSIBILITY

There are tremendous benefits to taking personal responsibility. On a personal level, it will give you a dramatic sense of empowerment over every element of your life. As a leader, it will significantly boost your credibility among those who follow you and every other constituent involved in your leadership role. Those in your organization will believe you and have confidence in you because they will see consistency and congruency in your words and behavior. It will make you more courageous than ever before, enabling you to make the tough calls and perform the tough tasks as well as take risks. So empowered, it will allow you to build a plan for success and, perhaps most importantly, create accountability in your organization.

> *Personal responsibility* is **the complete ownership of "what is."**

EXERCISE: TAKING PERSONAL RESPONSIBILITY

This exercise will launch you on your path toward complete responsibility. You will come to feel the power of knowing that you can affect events and conditions in your life, as opposed to feeling that you are a victim of them.

STEP 1: BE PRESENT

The foundational driver of presence, and the awareness and consciousness produced by it, is critical to the development of personal responsibility. Given that personal responsibility is the complete ownership of "what is," you must be firmly grounded in the home of "what is"—the present moment (see chapter 1). You must be in a condition that allows you to see your connection to everything around you.

STEP 2: IDENTIFY A MEANINGFUL EVENT OR CONDITION

Identify one event or condition in your life that had or is having a meaningful impact on the way you feel or live your life. It might be the accident you got into recently, when you were broadsided by another car driven by an uninsured motorist running a red light. On a much larger scale, it might be global warming. Or at work, you are unable to meet investors' expectations.

STEP 3: OWN THE EVENT OR CONDITION

Now, access the powerful driver of personal responsibility to own the event or condition you identified in step 2. No matter what it is, experiment with the idea that you are personally responsible. Say, "I am completely responsible for this event or condition in the following ways," and then list the ways. You may find yourself stretching for connections, but this is exactly the point. Most of us are not used to taking responsibility, so it feels like a stretch when we do it.

Let's look at some examples. Suppose you decide to take full responsibility for being broadsided by the car that ran the red light. You examine everything you could have done to contribute to the collision. You realize you drive too fast in general and drove too fast that afternoon while running errands. Had you driven slower, you would not have been there for the other driver to hit at that place and time. You realize you have run red lights on occasion, sometimes negligently and other times as you try to get through a yellow light before it turns red.

You realize you are too stressed, and without the stress you might have noticed the car approaching from the side with no evidence that it was going to stop. You realize you skipped lunch again and that, perhaps with better nutrition, you would have seen the car approaching and taken evasive action. You realize you were on your mobile phone at the time of the collision and maybe that contributed to not seeing the car. You realize your car sustained a substantial amount of damage and take this as a sign that you should be driving a car that is built better and has a better safety record.

As another example, suppose you take full responsibility for global warming. You examine everything you have done that could have contributed to it. You realize you drive a car that uses too much gas. You realize you drive too much. You realize you don't use public transportation enough. You realize you have not explored other means of transportation. You realize you heat your home too much in winter and could reduce your use of natural gas by wearing a sweater indoors in colder months. You realize you waste a lot of paper; this results in the use of more timber and fewer trees to convert carbon dioxide to oxygen. You realize you voted for the politicians who aren't seriously and decisively addressing the issue. You realize you own stock in an oil company.

Suppose you take full responsibility for your company's inability to meet investors' expectations. You seek every connection back to you. You ignore all other possible contributors to the event or condition. You realize your strategic vision was flawed. You realize you were too optimistic about your company's prospects and were wrong to convey that misplaced optimism to investors. You realize you organized your team in a way that it is insufficiently responsive to rapidly changing market conditions. You realize that you did not inspire maximum performance in your team members. You realize your system of accountability is flawed.

Sometimes the connections are elusive, but they are there. It might just take some openness and creativity to identify them. Remember from chapter 1 the discussion of the concept that for every action there is an equal and opposite reaction. If you really can find no connection, then start searching for a connection with something from your past. For example, suppose you are having a very difficult time engaging your team members in the pursuit of your organization's objective. You just can't find any justification for your difficulty under the present circumstances. Maybe in your past, however, you sold a company for the primary purpose of enriching yourself and the transaction was not a positive one for your team members at the time. Maybe this is the universe's way of balancing the scales. You were selfish once and got what you wanted to the detriment of your team. Now, when you are unselfish, you aren't getting what you want—or not getting it as easily as you normally would—to your own detriment.

With this exercise, you will gain a feeling of empowerment over the conditions and circumstances of your life. You will begin to feel that you could have done things differently to make them better. You will even begin to feel that you had a choice in them. Understanding your role in past events, you'll begin to understand how you can act to affect future events or conditions, instead of being at the mercy of them.

The objective in doing this is not to become a pitiful figure bearing the weight of the world's problems on your shoulders. It is not to blame yourself. Rather, the objective is to align yourself with "what is," develop an introspective awareness of your connection to everything around you, and discover a feeling of empowerment over your life.

The present moment is all there is. Everything outside of it—the past and the future—is not real. While there are some beneficial ways to think of the past or future, blaming others or denying responsibility is certainly not among them. They are merely escapes from the present, from "what is."

STEP 4: OWN YOUR RESPONSE

The final step in accessing the powerful driver of personal responsibility is to own your response to every event and condition in your life. In step 3, you took personal responsibility for the event or condition itself. Now you take responsibility for your response to it. This, in fact, is precisely the meaning of personal responsibility: your ability to respond. When you own your response, you choose your response. When you choose your response, you decide the effect the event or condition will have on your life. You are choosing to have control over your life. You are choosing to affect the world around you, instead of being its victim.

Blame, disownment, and neglect disempower you. Blaming, disowning, and neglecting are harmful thoughts, emotions, and behaviors, and you are the one being harmed. Your most empowering response will be a positive thought, emotion, or action. You make lemonade out of your pile of lemons.

Going back to the scenario where you were broadsided by a car running a red light, this step—owning your response—is the final "clearing out" of any negative energy associated with the event. You have already taken responsibility for being at the wrong place at the wrong time, and for being, perhaps, stressed, distracted, and undernourished. But you still feel depressed about the whole thing. In this step, you say, "Okay, it is what it is. It is over. I am left with some tasks to do—getting my car repaired, renting a car or finding other transportation, dealing with my insurance carrier—and I am going to do them in a timely manner with a positive attitude. I am going to write down all the things I have learned from this experience. Finally, I am going to be thankful for all good things—my health, my job, my friends—in my life."

The High-Impact Leader Empowered by Personal Responsibility: Evelyn

Evelyn is the principal of a middle school, which is in an economically challenged neighborhood. She was appointed three years ago. Immediately upon her appointment, she created and initiated a multifaceted program designed to increase the standardized test scores of her students, which were in the lowest quartile of the nation. After three years of a great amount of hard work, long hours, much patience, and dedication to her program, the scores hadn't increased a bit. In fact, they had declined slightly.

Evelyn could have blamed it on declining state funding. She could have blamed it on parental apathy. She could have blamed it on the local police chief's refusal to crack down on truancy and youth gang activity. She could have blamed it on the district's busing policy. She could have blamed it on her teachers, the teachers union, the students, or on the video games or rap music the students listen to. She could have blamed it on the tests themselves.

Evelyn could have blamed any number of people or conditions, but she didn't. Instead, she took complete personal responsibility. She stood up in front of a school board meeting, which was attended by the school district supervisor, most of her teachers, many parents, and, of course, all of the board members, and she took complete responsibility. She described in detail the program she had pursued for the past three years, and then provided in detail the disappointing history of test scores. She concluded by saying, "I take full responsibility for where we are. I hope I have described my program sufficiently for you to understand why I did the things I did and my sincerity in wanting to solve the performance problems of our students. But clearly my program has failed. And the failure is my responsibility. In failure, though, I have learned some things. These learnings, combined with input I will solicit from all constituents in the coming weeks, will lead to another, hopefully much more effective, program for significantly improving test scores. I will work very hard to make this happen. Those of you who know me know that this is a task I have never taken, and never will take, lightly."

No one called for her resignation. No one voiced criticism. Frankly, many constituents were relieved that criticism had not been directed their way. Teachers, parents, students, union leaders, and even board members knew in their hearts that they all shared some responsibility for the problem. Evelyn's willingness to shoulder full responsibility inspired members of each of those groups to assume some responsibility themselves. It is interesting how the assumption of personal responsibility creates a vacuum of sorts. When others see you shouldering the load, they step forward to assume some of the load themselves. None of this was articulated at the meeting, but it was felt. And it served as the seed for a broad-based alignment among constituents that Evelyn would need to support a much more aggressive program she was already envisioning.

Her credibility—her power of inspiring belief, combined with her worthiness of the confidence of others—increased dramatically. Anyone who will assume full responsibility must be believable, otherwise why would she or he assume it? No one wants to look bad. And doesn't someone who sounds very reasonable and intelligent and has the courage to absorb one of the most difficult consequences of leadership deserve our confidence?

In meetings that followed, the people whose cooperation she needed were more than willing to jump in her boat and grab an oar. They knew they had a leader who would assume the brunt of the chore. They knew they would never be publicly criticized. She had proven it right in front of their eyes. Teachers suggested new ideas for engaging students. The union agreed to soften their reaction to some teacher terminations that she felt were justified. Some parents offered to assist with an after-school tutoring program. Others agreed to contribute some money for some additional learning resources. Others volunteered to form a committee to create a "community code," which outlined parents' and students' commitment to the school's mission. The police chief agreed to devote more resources to the truancy and gang issues.

In the weeks that followed, Evelyn felt more courageous than ever before. The board meeting was the first time she had ever taken complete personal responsibility for something in a very public way. On past occasions, her fears would cause her to direct some blame elsewhere. But she found that she just became more fearful every time she did that. She worried more about job security. She worried more about failing. This time, however, she was almost overwhelmed with courage. If she could do what she had done at the board meeting, she could do anything. She could take any risk. She could accomplish anything. Her teachers and administrative staff saw her courage, and became more devoted than ever. They wanted to play on Evelyn's team.

Unexpectedly, Evelyn found herself more willing and capable of making the tough calls than ever before. She terminated the teachers whose performance was lacking. This further strengthened her credibility with the remaining hardworking teachers. For years, the hardworking teachers had known which teachers underperformed, and they resented the fact that those teachers earned the same salary as they did. Evelyn also went "toe-to-toe" with the president of the parent-teacher association, successfully arguing that the association had become virtually useless and that a new model of communication and collaboration was needed. She even found that students sensed her confidence and power and began engaging more in school activities.

She felt thoroughly empowered to build a plan for successfully increasing test scores because she felt she had more control than she had ever enjoyed. Three years before, she already had a lot of the ideas that she would now implement, but lacked the self-confidence, as well as the confidence and support of others, to implement them then. She found that when she assumed complete personal responsibility for a failure, it was much easier to assume complete responsibility for achieving success. In the absence of taking responsibility for failure, Evelyn would have always been out of alignment with reality—that is, if she had denied the reality of "what is," the reality of failure—she would not have been able to draw upon "what is" to achieve success.

Evelyn found that her ability to create a culture of accountability was dramatically enhanced. Her teachers and staff members felt compelled to meet her expectations for several reasons. First, she had defined her expectations more clearly than ever, feeling more empowered than ever. Second, they had seen her assume full personal responsibility and, as I mentioned, this assumption creates a vacuum that people want to fill with their own responsibility. Finally, they knew she would make the tough call, including terminating them, if the expectations were not met.

THE LEADERSHIP DASHBOARD

The Leadership Dashboard (figure 5.1) graphically demonstrates the impact of personal responsibility on a leader's ability to embody key character traits and perform critical leadership functions described in the introduction. It shows, on a 100-point scale, that built upon the foundation of presence, which allows you to see your role in every event and condition of your life, actively taking responsibility is powerful fuel that enables you to:

BE CREDIBLE. When you are personally responsible, by definition you are "walking the walk" and displaying consistency and congruency in your words and behavior.

BE COURAGEOUS. Once you have taken personal responsibility, making the tough calls, performing the tough tasks, and taking risks seems easy.

BUILD A PLAN. Personal responsibility provides you with a feeling of control and a belief that you can have an effect. You will find yourself more empowered than ever before to create and define the optimal path connecting vision to results.

CREATE ACCOUNTABILITY. When you, as a leader, take personal responsibility, you inspire your team members to take responsibility, and you support a culture and systems that require each individual to contribute his or her share.

Less so, but still in a powerful way, the driver of personal responsibility will also fuel your ability to:

BE SELF-DEFINED. Taking personal responsibility requires that you know your values, beliefs, higher purpose, and vision of the future, and express them clearly.

BE FORWARD THINKING. Personal responsibility forces you into a mode of creating your own future and that of your organization. You know that every future condition will be your responsibility and you would be foolish to stand on the sidelines as each evolves.

BE INSPIRING. Your personal responsibility, in the way it inspires others to assume their own, greatly assists your ability to define your vision in a way that your team members see themselves in it.

BE PEOPLE-ORIENTED. The awareness you achieve through your presence—an awareness that is your personal responsibility to develop—enhances your people skills by revealing the value in people around you and your connection to them.

BE SUPPORTIVE. When you are fully conscious and personally responsible for everything in your life, and when you have an organizational objective to achieve, you have no option but to optimize the strength of your team by fostering an environment that encourages risk taking, collaboration, self-leadership, and recognition, and that facilitates the transformation of challenges into personal growth.

BUILD A VALUES-BASED CORE. When you have put your own personal stake in the ground that "this is who I am; this is what I stand for; and every event and condition in my life is my responsibility," it is natural for the organization to drive its own collective stake in the ground.

FORM A VISION. For the same reason that personal responsibility fuels your ability to be forward thinking, it forces you to transform ideas and possibilities into an organizational objective.

ENGAGE A TEAM. People want to work with a leader who takes complete personal responsibility. They are inspired to take responsibility for their share of accomplishing the organizational vision.

PRODUCE RESULTS. When you have no one to blame for a result different from the one you want, you tend to produce the one you want.

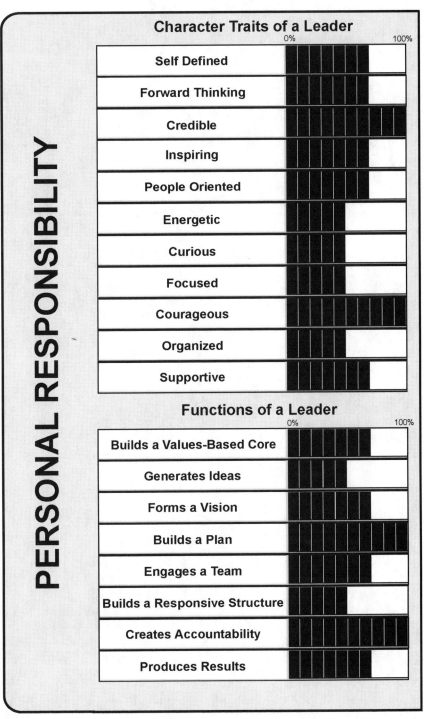

FIGURE 5.1

CHAPTER 6

INTUITION
The Sixth Driver of the
High-Impact Leader

Hunch, gut feeling, impression, psychic hit—these are all names for this power called intuition. *Intuition* is a tool for acquiring knowledge without the process of rational thought. It is the sixth sense; it is what informs you beyond the first five senses of taste, hearing, touch, smell, and sight. I've always liked Laura Day's definition in *Practical Intuition*: she describes intuition as "knowing without knowing why you know" (Day 1997, 81). Each of us has it, and each of us can develop it to powerful levels.

What is the source of this knowledge? Simply put, the universe. It is everything you have ever experienced or known. In fact, it is everything humankind has experienced or known. Carl Jung (1959), the famous Swiss psychiatrist, conducted extensive studies and concluded that there is a "collective unconscious" that is common to every person. This collective unconscious is essentially a library of human experience into which any of us can tap at any time.

> *Intuition* **is a tool for acquiring knowledge without the process of rational thought.**

This chapter addresses the rise and fall, and imminent rise again, of intuition. You'll learn how to develop your intuition and make it a powerful driver that fuels your ability as a leader to define yourself; inspire your team; form the optimal, compelling vision for your organization; and assemble a responsive structure to execute that vision.

THE FIRST RISE OF INTUITION

At some point in the millions of years of human evolution, the human brain developed a capacity for intuition. This capacity is in the right side of the brain, whereas our rational, logical capabilities reside in the left side. The right side of the brain is inward focused, fueled from deep within. The left is externally focused, fueled by external data. Until the last two centuries, we humans relied upon intuition as heavily as we relied upon our other five senses. We were "balanced-brain beings."

Think about a world where the only data you could access is that which you perceived through your tongue, ears, skin, nose, and eyes. Physically, you were limited by how far your feet would carry you. In your effort to survive, you undoubtedly relied greatly on rational thought and your left brain. You saw rain clouds gathering on the horizon, sensed cooler temperatures and higher humidity on your skin, and deduced that rain was likely and you better bring in the meat that was drying on racks outside your cave.

But the amount of data that could be perceived through your five senses and fed into your rational thought processes was so limited that you also relied greatly upon the nonlogical senses in your right brain— that is, you relied on your intuition. You may have felt the presence of valuable water beyond a distant mountain. Long before you saw or heard anything, you likely felt the threat of an approaching pack of predatory animals. Simply by seeing the silhouette of a stranger approaching in the distance, you may have sensed he was from a friendly tribe and thus meant no harm. In fact, in shamanic cultures, going back tens of thousands of years, the greater your intuition, the more likely you were to be the tribal leader and healer.

THE FALL OF INTUITION

During the past two hundred years, however, most people became primarily left-brain beings. As the velocity and complexity of life accelerated, we humans focused outward. This change was not due to a conscious choice; we were simply overwhelmed by the external world. With very little time to ground ourselves amid the onslaught of external data, we lost confidence in intuition. We came to rely disproportionately on rational thinking.

TECHNOLOGY

Ever so insidiously, technological advances opened up data channels, or means of exchanging information. They began to overfeed our left brains. First, we progressed from travel by foot and riding on the backs of animals to engine-powered vehicles. We were able to cover a lot more ground and, as a result, gather more data to feed our left brains. Then, in the nineteenth and twentieth centuries, we developed the telegraph, telephone, typewriter, calculator, radio, television, audio recorder, video recorder, fax machine, mobile phone, and, of course, the personal computer, and the Internet. Today the velocity and complexity of our lives has become overwhelming. Most of us are literally being flooded with data, which our left brains must process. We simply don't have time to fully use our right brain and, specifically, its powerful ability to intuit. Intuition as a tool has largely been crowded out of our existence. It still exists, of course. We have each experienced the first impression that proved to be absolutely correct. Yet we just don't have the time or energy to use or develop our intuition. And because we don't use it much, we don't trust it much.

CHILDHOOD CONDITIONING

As technology began to change the shape of industry in the nineteenth century, industry began to change the shape of families and education. As men and women began working away from their homes and

135

farms, the education of children changed from homeschooling to collective education. Schools began to proliferate, and more children left home each day to go to school. To effectively manage education, teachers and administrators, understandably, increasingly relied upon objective tools. In particular, they increasingly relied upon tests, with right and wrong answers. The quest for the right answer became paramount. Parents bought into it, unconsciously I'm sure, in an effort to stay on top of their children's progress without investing too much time out of their busy days. The result was that the left brain, home to the thinking process necessary to formulate a "right" answer, or to distinguish between a right and wrong answer, increased in importance vis-à-vis the right brain.

Social Conditioning

As discussed in chapter 5, another phenomenon of recent history is the development of a culture that discourages personal responsibility. Our governments, court systems, and religions encourage many of us to believe we are without power. Many of us believe our lives are determined by other people and forces beyond our control. With the pervasiveness of this belief, it is easy to see why we ignore and distrust this powerful driver of intuition that burns inside of us. We feel these outside forces have control over us, and they want "correct"—objectively defined and verifiable—behavior from us. We'd better provide that behavior or we will suffer.

What if I, the head of a regional office of a multinational company, closed the office one day and gave everyone a holiday because I had a gut feeling that productivity on that day, for reasons I could not quantify or even rationally explain, would be so low that it wouldn't justify opening, or that a holiday would boost morale such that future productivity would increase disproportionately to the cost of the holiday? Chances are that I would be ridiculed and perhaps even reprimanded by my superiors. They believe that my ability to positively affect conditions is limited and is prescribed in their policies and procedures, and any attempt to affect conditions outside of those limitations is discouraged. And most people buy into their limitations because they do not want to risk a reprimand or other negative consequence. As a result, most people suffer a diminished sense of personal responsibility and, of course, have a lesser ability to positively affect conditions in their lives.

FACT ADDICTION

Somewhere along the way, in our pursuit of the "right" answer, many of us became addicted to facts. Indeed, we associate "facts" with virtue and rightness. Many think that those armed with facts are more credible, indeed better, than the unarmed. We built a system of criminal and civil justice that depends first upon identifying facts and then applying law to those facts. We extended the mentality, and indeed the process, far beyond the courtroom. Kids taunt each other with expressions like, "You can't prove it!" Parents interrogate their kids to discover the facts, so they can determine who is right and who is wrong, and who should be punished and who rewarded. When there is trouble at school, teachers vow to "get to the bottom of it." This continues all the way through to the most sophisticated levels of human activity, where anything uttered on Wall Street, at a biotech convention, or in the U.S. Senate must be validated by verifiable "facts" or it is discredited.

But what is a fact? It is a mere snapshot of reality. As a snapshot, it is limited in time, range, and context. First, it is only valid as of the time of the snapshot. What existed at the moment of the snapshot is now different and will be different again at every moment going forward. Second, the snapshot only captures a limited range of reality at the time of the snapshot, and its value is maximized only where we can understand it in the context of everything outside of its range. While I may try hard to document the reality outside of the snapshot, it is impossible for me to really know everything that existed outside the range.

Let's say I head up a U.S. car manufacturer. You tell me you surveyed all car owners in the country for their preferences, and found the overwhelming majority loves hybrid vehicles and would like to buy one. Well, the data was good at the time the survey was conducted, but it is now stale. Maybe demand for hybrids has gone up, and maybe it has gone down, but it is certainly not identical to what it was at the time of the survey. Moreover, an infinite number of outside conditions might have had an effect on the survey, such as the price of oil, the threat of war in the Middle East, consumer confidence, household savings rates, fashion trends, superior technologies under development, and the phrasing of the survey questions. In reality, the "facts" that seem to indicate a strong demand for hybrids may be illusory in this moment.

Nevertheless, many of us are addicted to facts. We fill up our left brains with them and crowd out the ability of our right brains to exercise some influence on what we believe and how we behave.

THE MEGA-SIZED ORGANIZATION

Two hundred years ago, outside of military forces, organized religion, and political or governmental bodies, few large organizations existed. And even where large organizations did exist, the lack of technology meant that leaders of businesses, government entities, social organizations, and educational institutions directly interacted with the people in their organizations and those whom the organization served. People looked into the eyes of other people who affected their lives.

With the booming human population and our creation of the Industrial Revolution and Information Age, large organizations have increased dramatically in both number and in size. Today leaders of large organizations are often far removed from both the members of their organization and the people—such as customers, suppliers, and shareholders—who influence the organization from the outside. They create policy and then employ multitudes of people to execute it. They control the behavior of their employees the only way they know how—through objective means. Performance and productivity are measured, weighed, and analyzed. Just as there is little room for personal contact in an efficient mega-organization, there is also little room for intuition.

INTUITION RISES AGAIN

Ironically, like the nutrient-rich ashes from which the phoenix rose, the primary cause of intuition's fall—technology and the resulting flood of data pouring into our left brains—is fueling its revival. We are overwhelmed with data. We are confused. We are tired. We are ungrounded.

We are not making better decisions than we used to. We are not behaving better.

We need to find an anchor in the storm—an anchor that will help us manage the data better and with less stress, an anchor that will make the data more relevant and thus help us make better decisions and behave better, an anchor that will bring us closer to reality, that will ground us and rejuvenate us. That anchor is intuition.

TYPES OF INTUITIVE CUES

I think of *intuitive cues* as conduits for reality. They are simply how we receive our "signal" of reality. There is a reality, either outside or within us, that is trying to express itself to us. Our responsibility is to ensure that the channels are open and clear so that the reality can be seen, experienced, and utilized in a positive way. If the productivity of my team is going to be abysmal tomorrow, I have a responsibility to ensure, or at least maximize the chance, that I learn of this ahead of time. What tools are available to me? Several types of intuitive cues exist—clairsentience, clairvoyance, clairaudience, and just plain knowing—but none is better than the others. Each of us generally has a "preferred" cue—that is, one that comes more naturally than others—but, with some attention and effort, we can develop all of the cues and utilize their power.

CLAIRSENTIENCE. *Clairsentience* is feeling something in your body. Have you ever experienced a tightening in your chest when your boss called you and said, "Can you come see me as soon as you can?" You just knew, without any data, that he was going to communicate something negative to you. The tone of his voice didn't indicate it. His words alone didn't necessarily indicate it. But you knew something negative was going to happen. Sure enough, he informed you that the company was reorganizing and you would now be reporting to someone with whom you had never gotten along.

In response to the same call, maybe you experienced a racing heart and excitement. You just knew that he was going to communicate something positive. Sure enough, he informed you that you were being promoted in pay, title, and responsibility because of the great work you had done.

Clairsentience is fed by the reality of your environment. If someone close to you is feeling a strong emotion, you feel it. If someone close to you is ill, you feel it. If you are in physical danger, you feel it. You feel a reality, even though you cannot objectively prove it.

CLAIRVOYANCE. *Clairvoyance* is seeing something, an image, in your mind's eye. We can all conjure the vision of a psychic closing her eyes, with her hands on a crystal ball, and describing a vision of what she sees in her head. But clairvoyance is not the exclusive property of the professional seer. We all have mental visions, or can have visions if we are open enough, of a reality just as real as that which we see with our eyes. A fellow with whom I once worked on a transaction kept having visions of having an operation, recovering well, and being joyful about the experience. About a year after the onset of his visions, his mother's kidneys failed. At the time his visions began, he knew nothing about his mother's kidney disease. He ended up donating one of his own kidneys to his mother. He believes that his vision gave him partial insight to, and helped prepare him for, this very challenging situation and major decision.

CLAIRAUDIENCE. *Clairaudience* is hearing something in your head. Sometimes clairaudience reveals your own inner voice, and sometimes the voice of another. When I worked in investment banking, I remember a trader telling me that he knew when to buy when the voice inside his head yelled "Buy!!" and when to sell when it screamed "Sell!!" Hundreds of millions of dollars were exchanged each day based on his clairaudience, and very successfully. He always had some data in which to cloak his decision, but the decision was made by the voice in his head.

JUST PLAIN KNOWING. Finally, there are times that you can't feel anything, see anything, or hear anything, but you just know something deep in your heart. I experience this cue more than the others. I just know that a particular business will be successful. I just know when another will fail. I just know that a particular job candidate will be a successful hire. I just know that another will not.

THE HIGHEST AND BEST USES OF INTUITION

Intuition should not be used in a vacuum. At least I would never use it alone. My intuitive skills are just not advanced enough—and likely never will be—to depend upon them to the exclusion of external data and logical thinking. Likewise, intuition should never be ignored. At a minimum, intuition is a tool to be used in conjunction with all other input in the decision-making process. At certain times, however, intuition can be dominant, including the following:

WHEN RELEVANT FACTS ARE SCARCE OR CONFLICTING. Many times we find ourselves in a position of having insufficient facts, facts that conflict with each other, or facts that are old or inapplicable. This is the time to turn to intuition for direction.

WHEN WE JUST CAN'T DECIDE AMONG ALTERNATIVES. At other times, we are just plain undecided. We can't make a decision. We line up the pros and cons, we weigh them, and we analyze them ad nauseum, but we still can't decide. Intuition, in my experience, always provides the answer, and always the right one. We may fight our intuition, stacking all the objective data against it and arguing why our intuition is wrong, but intuition, in my experience, is always correct.

WHEN UNDER TIME PRESSURE. Intuition is a perfect tool, indeed the only tool, when there is time pressure to act or react and the data does not provide a clear course. I believe the old adage that if something is too good to be true, it usually isn't true. But there have been times in my career when I was presented with an "urgent" opportunity to pursue something that promised a huge windfall, and the possibility of the windfall got me salivating as I considered the opportunity. I knew in my heart that the opportunity was very risky, the windfall was very uncertain, or the people involved were less than professional, but the size of the potential windfall made me think hard. At those times, I always went with my intuition and, to my knowledge, not one of the opportunities I passed on ever amounted to anything.

141

WHEN DEALING WITH HUMAN ISSUES. Intuition is critical when dealing with human issues, such as hiring, firing, staffing, and partnering.

> Intuition is a perfect tool, indeed the only tool, when there is time pressure to act or react and the data does not provide a clear course.

Objective facts are very important, but as a final determinant at "crunch time," they just don't compete with our intuitive ability to assess another human being. I have hired people with extraordinarily impressive resumés, over intuitive objections, only to have them flame out. Likewise, I have hired extraordinary employees who had only lukewarm resumés but strong intuitive appeal.

INTUITION MUST BE FED

Some people may be inclined to ask, "With this powerful intuition, do I really have to study all the data anymore? Do I really have to use all that logic in my left brain anymore? Why can't intuition be my sole guide?"

The answer is that intuition is not an isolated, self-contained, perpetual power that operates on its own energy. In fact, there is no such energy. Everything, including intuition, needs its own energy source or sources. And the energy source for intuition is external input perceived by the other five senses and rationally processed by the left brain. The more input of this energy, the more effectively intuition operates.

The most intuitive leaders I know have voracious appetites for information. They read scores of general news and trade publications, and a wide variety of literature and other books; they interact frequently with a diverse group of friends, acquaintances, and mentors; they listen to and watch a wide variety of news and other programs, and have rich and diverse tastes in music, theater, film, and recreational activities. They understand, indeed live, the powerful feedback loop of intuition: they feed their minds and souls, listen to and are guided by intuition, experience the increased contentment and leadership effectiveness that results, and then seek out more fuel for their minds and souls.

EXERCISE:
INTUITIVE PROCESSING

We all have intuition. The intuition of some is just naturally strong. Most of us, however, have to make a deliberate effort to develop its strength. This intuitive process exercise is an excellent way to develop your intuition. As with anything, it takes intention to make intuition a powerful guide in your life. It takes time. You already devote a tremendous amount of time to rational thinking. You'll need to reallocate a small portion of that time to intuitive processing. It takes openness, which you already started developing in chapter 2. It takes patience. You may have spent a lifetime distancing yourself from your intuitive capability, and you need to take some time to get reacquainted with it. Probably more than anything else, though, developing your intuition requires trust. You must trust that, after some solid work, it will provide you with better guidance than you have ever had.

On a personal level, intuitive processing will dramatically build your self-confidence and help you make better choices in all areas of your life. On a leadership level, it will take the grounding that you accomplished with your practice of presence to a significantly deeper level. It will allow you to tap into a deeper source of knowledge than you have ever known. Your ability to define yourself will be enhanced because you will understand yourself better. Your ability to inspire will be enhanced because you will have a much better understanding of the most compelling and unifying common purpose and how to communicate it so that your team members see themselves in it. You will be able to form the optimal vision for your organization because you have tapped into and been guided by the most reliable source of data, the universal stream of knowledge and experience. Finally, you will know, sometimes in ways that defy rational explanation, how to structure your organization so that it responds efficiently to our complex, dynamic environment.

Before you begin this exercise, it's important to recognize that intuition is constantly at work providing you with knowledge outside your rational thought process. "Psychic hits" are streamed to you continually. They are reflected in thoughts such as "I think I'll knock off work now; I've had enough for the day" or "I think I'll take the alternate way home from work tonight." You follow this intuitive guidance much of the time

143

but in relatively mundane matters. With such mundane matters, intuition doesn't have to be managed formally. It knows how to take care of you without a lot of your conscious help.

When the importance of the decision, issue, challenge, or relationship is greater, however, your intuitive capabilities need active management to provide you with meaningful guidance. This exercise will help you actively manage your intuition to gain the fullest benefit from it. Also, the clearer your mind, the easier it will be to perceive intuitively. Thus, a regular practice of meditation is the best foundation for developing your intuition. In my experience, people who meditate are far more intuitive than those who don't, even if they do nothing formal to develop their intuition. Meditation (see chapter 1) immediately preceding this exercise is especially beneficial.

STEP 1: POSE A QUESTION

Pose a question that is clear, specific, and unambiguous. Make it as easy as you can on your intuition. It wants to answer your question but needs to completely understand precisely what it is you are asking. Write your question in your journal, repeat it several times aloud, with complete focus and attention.

I once worked with a lawyer who was in the middle of a highly successful career, yet he kept feeling that perhaps there was a better course for him in life. He couldn't think of anything in particular, but just couldn't shake the feeling. When he did this intuitive processing exercise, this is the simple question he posed: Should I be practicing law? He didn't ask, Will I be happier if I stop practicing law? Or will I be able to provide for my family if I stop practicing law? Or what types of things should I be looking to do if I stop practicing law? He simply asked, Should I be practicing law?

STEP 2: IDENTIFY THE GUIDING LANGUAGE

Intuition does not speak the rational language of the left brain. It uses symbols, images, and metaphors. Fortunately, it suggests to you the symbols, images, and metaphors that will be most appropriate for communication. Your job is simply to hear the suggestion. You'll know when you've heard it because it will just feel right. Then prepare your mind to communicate in that language.

For instance, if you have a choice of alternatives in front of you, you might be drawn to an image of a path that diverges in several directions, with each path representing an alternative. Or you might be attracted to an image of several doors in front of you or perhaps a set of boxes.

If you are contemplating a broader question, where the alternatives are not clear to you, a more expansive image might be appropriate. You might imagine yourself walking or driving down a road. You might imagine yourself entering a house or other building. You might see yourself on a movie screen. You might see yourself as a character in a book. You might imagine you are a tree, and every root, limb, and leaf will inform you. This will take a little bit of practice, but in no time you will have a set of scenarios, one of which will work for you in any situation, whether you are contemplating a decision, issue, challenge, or relationship.

The lawyer I mentioned above imagined himself as an oak tree because an oak tree was just what kept coming to his mind. He tried to envision himself on a freeway, in an old house with many rooms, and even swimming in the ocean, but he kept coming back to the oak tree. He wasn't sure where the guiding image would take him, but he knew it was the right one.

STEP 3: RECEIVE THE ANSWER

There are five parts to the process of receiving an answer:

■ Prepare for intuition processing

■ Begin to relax

■ Relax progressively

■ Picture a peaceful, pleasant scene

■ Allow your image to guide you

PREPARE FOR INTUITION PROCESSING

To prepare yourself to receive the answer, allocate twenty or thirty minutes in which you will not be disturbed. Find a quiet, comfortable space. Avoid the bed because it is too easy to fall asleep. Rather, sit on a chair, meditation bench, or cushion on the floor. Sit erect and try not to lean backward against the seat back; slumping backward against a rest tends to induce sleep. Just as in meditation, an erect posture with chin slightly tucked is ideal.

If you are in a chair, place your bare feet firmly on the floor. If on a meditation cushion or bench, cross your legs or tuck them under or beside you (toes pointing behind you), again keeping your spine erect. There are many different hand positions. Try different ones until you find one that works for you. I usually open my hands and face my palms upward. Then close your eyes.

BEGIN TO RELAX

Close your mouth and start to breathe through your nose. As you draw in your breath, fully experience it. Feel the coolness of the air as it passes through your nostrils and starts to fill your lungs. Feel your chest expand with oxygen. Feel its essential nature—it is your lifeblood. As you exhale, feel your chest contract. Feel the warmth of your breath as it passes through your nostrils.

After two or three minutes of this, begin a progressive relaxation.

RELAX PROGRESSIVELY

Focus your attention on your toes and feel them relax completely. When they feel relaxed, focus on the ball of your foot. When that is relaxed, move to your instep, and so on up your legs and body until your entire body is completely relaxed. Sometimes this progressive relaxation may take awhile in the learning stages, but with experience comes speed. Soon you'll be relaxed in two or three minutes.

PICTURE A PEACEFUL, PLEASANT SCENE

Now picture yourself in the most pleasant scene you can conjure up in your mind. Something peaceful, serene, safe, and beautiful—perhaps you're on a bluff overlooking the ocean on a beautiful day, or you're in a peaceful meadow surrounded by lush trees.

ALLOW YOUR IMAGE TO GUIDE YOU

Once you feel immersed in your setting, restate your question from step 1. Then recall the image you selected in step 2 and allow the image to lead you. It is critical here that you only observe. Form no judgments and make no interpretations. Now is the time to stop trying. Just allow your intuition to speak to you in its sometimes cryptic, scattered, meandering way.

After awhile, usually not more than fifteen or twenty minutes, the scene will have played out and nothing new will arise. This is your intuition's signal that its message has been communicated as best as it can be and this part of the exercise is over.

When the lawyer came to this part of step 3, he first saw himself as an old but very healthy oak tree. He was solid. People sought shelter under his expanse. He was drawn to follow his roots deep into the ground. He felt water and first interpreted it as a healthy sign. He was tempted to leave the roots and explore the branches when he realized that there was too much water. It was pooling around his root network and had rotted the deeper portions of the roots. He perceived the rot moving upward, slowly and insidiously.

Above ground, he felt quite uncomfortable. He saw a construction site adjacent to him. The activity had stirred up a lot of dirt that had settled on his leaves and deprived him of light and oxygen. He felt as if he were suffocating. His branches and leaves were a tangled mess, and they felt dry and brittle.

STEP 4: RECORD

In your journal, jot down everything you can recall about the images you experienced in step 3. Again, make no judgments or interpretations. Just try to recall every detail you observed, without addition.

The lawyer described how he'd first seen himself as an oak tree and how that image evolved. He noted that in addition to the tree image, he'd been presented with a new image—a construction site—and he noted how that image interacted with his original image: dirt from the construction settled on his leaves, depriving him of light and oxygen. He felt suffocated, and that his dry, brittle leaves were a tangled mess.

STEP 5: INTERPRET

The objective here is to try to find meaning and guidance in the images you observed and recorded without judgment or interpretation in steps 3 and 4. At last, you get to use your old friend, the left side of your brain! You'll allow the left side of the brain to exercise its logic and associative skills, but under the guidance of the right brain. You don't want the left to dominate and close you off to the reality that your right side is trying to show you.

Again, restate your question from step 1. Make sure your intuition is clear about what you are seeking. Then begin to interpret. In this step, I usually write my interpretations. Some people verbally record them. Sometimes, however, writing or recording just gets in the way and you need to, in the vernacular of musicians, just let your mind "riff," or take over and lead you. However you do it, start to make sense out of the data you just collected in step 3. Allow your mind to brainstorm for interpretations. Allow one interpretation to prompt another. Identify associations and other significant meanings and relationships. Don't become attached to one over the other, at least initially. Just let them develop.

As you interpret, continually remind your intuition of your question and the fact that you are only concerned about information that is relevant to that question. There are three significant challenges in this step, each of which can be overcome with awareness and practice:

1. Hopes and fears will appear in the disguise of relevant intuitive data. Let's say you are a chief executive officer and are contemplating hiring a new chief operating officer. Three candidates appear equally qualified and you just can't decide whom to hire. In this step, you notice several negative images arise around one candidate. You might at first say that your intuition has spoken and he must be eliminated from contention. But the negative images might emanate from your own fears about ultimately being replaced as chief executive by this candidate. They might stem from your projections about his personality that, upon closer examination, reflect more about your own personality.

   There is no easy solution to this issue. But the more present and open you are, the more clarity you have in your emotions and behavior, the more personal responsibility you take for the events and conditions in your life, and the more you consciously develop your intuition, the easier this challenge will be to meet.

2. The rational mind will attempt to interfere with the process. You believe it has served you well in the past, and it has a powerful yearning to not only survive, but thrive. The key is to use it, but don't overuse it. Again, the more you have developed the key drivers described in this book, the easier it will be to overcome this challenge by your rational mind.

3. Intuition involves possibilities, not certainties. It suggests alternatives, solutions, and answers. It provides you with important data, but it doesn't hit you over the head with a recommendation. It is up to you to internalize the data, hear the suggestions, and then use your free choice to act in accordance with or contrary to those suggestions. This presents a challenge to most of us who have spent a lifetime using our left brains in an effort to find absolutes. Practice, again, makes this challenge very manageable.

Not surprisingly, the lawyer with whom I worked didn't have much trouble interpreting the images that arose around his oak tree. He felt he was perceived as the solid, protective oak tree in the lives of his wife, children, partners, and employees. But the reality underneath this perception was that he felt as if he were slowly drowning in the role. Beyond just not being nourished by his practice, he felt as if he were rotting from deep within. The external world couldn't see it, but it was only a matter of time before it would.

He interpreted the adjacent construction site as everything his practice was not: productive, dynamic, bold, and self-determined. The dust arising from it and coating his leaves was like salt in a wound. The parched, fragile, and tangled branches and leaves represented a life lived not in alignment with his inner purpose and ultimately signified a slow death.

STEP 6: VERIFY

If you are fortunate, like the lawyer, your question was undeniably answered in step 5; you have no doubts about it. In most cases, though, some validation of your interpretation will be useful. The objective here is to be creative in how you go about it and honest in assessing what you find.

1. Look for objectively verifiable facts. Everything in this process may scream at you to go build an office building at an incredibly well-located site in your town. When you look for relevant facts, though, you might find that a gas station was a prior tenant and there are millions of dollars of environmental damage to the site, and scores of lawsuits. Was your intuition wrong? I don't think it is ever wrong. I believe it is only used improperly or suboptimally. In this case, the question of whether to build the office building should never have been posed to your intuition. It could easily have been answered by your left brain much earlier.

   If you find that objective facts do not contradict your intuition, you are in good shape. If you find facts that do contradict your intuition, and you just can't seem to shake the feeling that the intuition is incorrect, this becomes a new intuition. You can go through the process again, and may well reach a different result.

2. Discuss your interpretations with mentors or advisors. We all have them, or should have them. These people provide us candid and solid advice when we need it. Their word shouldn't be the last, but consulting them is a useful and sometimes necessary step that provides us with either the courage to act upon our intuition or to acknowledge that it may have been unduly influenced by a hope, fear, or the rational thought process.

3. To the extent time allows, let your intuitive guidance sit for a while. The situation will determine how long is appropriate, but just imagine for a day or two that you are now living as your intuition guided you and see how it feels. If it feels pretty good and you have the feeling in your heart that your intuition was correct, great. But if it is not feeling good, then you should begin the process over again, perhaps refining the question. The first effort will not have been wasted. It will feed your intuition the next time around, and you will feel better about the result of that subsequent process.

My lawyer friend discussed his intuition with his spouse and a number of his close friends, including some lawyers. He found that they were in unanimous agreement with his intuition. They thought he could be happier, and even earn a higher income, leaving the practice of law and joining an operating company. He then just sat on the consideration for a couple months. With each day in that period, however, he became more convinced that his intuition was correct. In fact, he reached a level of complete certainty.

STEP 7: ACT

To build confidence in your intuition and start to exploit the extraordinary transformative power it contains, it is important to act upon the intuitive guidance. If your intuition tells you to make a choice, make the choice and live with it. If it tells you to handle a challenge in a certain way, handle it that way and live with it. If it tells you to approach an issue in a certain way, approach it that way and live with it. If it tells you to act in a relationship in a certain way, act and live with it.

Action for the lawyer whose story we've been following meant changing jobs. Less than six months after doing this exercise, he joined a medical device company as an in-house attorney. This was a first step toward building a strong base of business experience, which eventually led to his starting his own company.

STEP 8: RECORD

After taking action, keep a record in your journal of your interpretation, verification, the action you took, the result, and how you feel about the result. Over time, you'll undoubtedly see patterns emerge that will help develop your intuition even more.

The High-Impact Leader Empowered by Intuition: Vern Raburn

After a very successful career as a senior executive with a number of high-tech companies including Microsoft, Symantec, and Lotus Development, Vern Raburn found himself in 1997 with some time on his hands. As with most dynamic, accomplished leaders, time on Vern's hands meant something of value was going to be created.

A pilot since the age of seventeen, Vern saw an opportunity in aviation to combine his technical expertise with his love of flying. He studied the commercial airline industry in the United States and concluded that it was nearing capacity. He found that the great majority of airline traffic was squeezing through about twenty hubs. For consumers, this meant airline travel was really only convenient for travel between hub cities.

Given the weak financial condition of airlines, the growing scarcity of public funds for hub development and expansion, and environmental challenges, he believed there wouldn't be any major expansion to the hub system in the foreseeable future. So, how would consumers be served as use neared capacity?

He knew there were over ten thousand small, local airports that were not heavily used. He also knew that the small airplanes that used those airports could not be relied upon to supplement the hub system and ease the capacity issues because they were either too expensive or too slow. His vision: a small, high-speed jet (since dubbed Very Light Jet or VLJ by the company he ultimately formed) that could be built for a fraction of the cost of a comparable performance jet. The jet would be both highly reliable and highly efficient to operate and maintain. On a grander scale, he envisioned a nationwide network of these jets providing highly convenient air service to thousands of destinations.

But how could he build a small, high-speed jet at a cost low enough to make his vision realistic? Well, the first thing Vern did was ignore the experts. Instead, he consulted his intuition, just as he had done throughout his successful career. The experts said several other very established companies, including Cessna and Raytheon, knew a lot about building small jets and couldn't produce one that could sell for less than $4.5 million. But his gut told him that he could incorporate technology from other industries and dramatically reduce costs.

So he went about it. In 1998, he formed Eclipse Aviation. In 1999, he raised $60 million from wealthy friends, including Microsoft founder Bill Gates. From the ground up, he looked for more efficient ways to build a jet. Intent on success, he designed his company for volume production. He used standardized production techniques and highly standardized machined parts everywhere he could. Instead of rivets that are production-time hogs, he used "friction stir welding" technology—never used before in passenger-jet production—to join aluminum panels. He stuck to his core competency, design and assembly, and outsourced every component he could without sacrificing his cost and quality objectives.

Since 1999, he has raised hundreds of millions of dollars, built a team of 850 employees, partnered with scores of suppliers, and, on September 30, 2006, was granted approval by the

Federal Aviation Administration to produce and sell the world's first VLJs. The Eclipse 500 will retail for $1.5 million, fly 425 miles per hour at altitudes up to 41,000 feet and for distances of up to 1,300 miles, and have the lowest operating cost per mile of any jet on the market. In addition, it can land at over ten thousand airports in the United States. He has firm orders for over 2,500 jets.

To his credit, a new industry-within-an-industry was born. Other companies have jumped on the bandwagon and are aggressively developing their own VLJs. As a result of his vision and efforts, we are substantially closer to having, for the first time, a national network of small jets providing highly convenient, affordable air travel between thousands of locations. While perhaps not of the magnitude of the Wright Brothers' invention of the first flying machine, the Eclipse 500 already ranks as one of the most significant technological advances in aviation history. I suspect it will rank as one of the most important advances in the history of commercial aviation.

Vern credits intuition or, as he describes it, "being able to see the answers without going through the process" with much of his leadership success in general and to the success of Eclipse Aviation in particular. Intuition fuels his vision of the future and his ability to express it clearly. He knew the "experts" were wrong. He knew his vision for Eclipse could be realized.

Intuition drives his ability to build and inspire his team. First, he relies upon it in hiring the right people. "Resumés are a good starting point, but give me an hour to interact with someone, and my intuition will give me a better read of a person than I could get anywhere else." Second, he relies upon it in determining when a person is not fitting into his team as he would like, and what to do about it. Finally, he relies upon it, probably more than anything else, in making the tough calls— those courageous, difficult, fateful decisions and actions that ultimately define the high-impact leader and seal the confidence of his team: We will commit to these design and development deadlines. We will replace this key supplier with that one. We will reassign this engineer, let that one go, and promote this other one.

He also credits intuition for his ability to build a responsive structure that is aligned with an environment of uncertainty, complexity, and rapid change, and not inordinately vulnerable to devastating mistakes. As Vern puts it, "The best leader uses a combination of right-brain intuition and left-brain logical thinking, and knows when to use each. Sole reliance on left-brain logical thinking is dangerous. It can lead you down false paths and headlong into bad situations, often after it is too late to do anything about it. Intuition works the other way. It tells me, and very reliably, how to avoid big mistakes."

Like all high-impact leaders I have known, Vern is a big fan of using mentors to help him flesh out and articulate his intuition. He often finds, particularly with the most difficult issues, that the process of explaining the issue to people he trusts and respects—in essence, teaching the issue and his intuition about it—galvanizes the intuition within him.

THE LEADERSHIP DASHBOARD

The Leadership Dashboard (figure 6.1) graphically demonstrates how the high-impact leader uses the powerful driver of intuition to dramatically enhance certain leadership character traits and functions. It shows, on a 100-point scale, that intuition provides you with a "knowingness" beyond your five other senses and rational thought that enables you to:

BE SELF-DEFINED. Intuition, with its inward-focused right-brain genesis, is the key to intimately knowing your values, beliefs, higher purpose, and vision of the future, and being able to express them clearly.

BE INSPIRING. Intuition allows you to listen deeply to others to discover a common purpose, and then give life to your vision by communicating it so that your team members see themselves in it.

FORM A VISION. Left-brain thinking—rational thought—is a commodity. As such, it produces a commodity product, a rational vision, with commodity pricing. Intuition, by definition, allows you to reach beyond

155

commodity vision and process ideas and possibilities into a highly valuable organizational objective.

BUILD A RESPONSIVE STRUCTURE. Intuition and its powerful insight enable you to build a structure ideally suited for the dynamic, high velocity, highly complex, interconnected world in which we live. This permeable structure is highly adaptive and responsive to changing conditions.

Less so, but still powerfully, intuition also fuels your ability to:

BE FORWARD THINKING. Intuition, and your trust in your intuition, empowers you to envision infinite possibilities.

BE CREDIBLE. No one inspires more confidence in others, or is perceived by others as more competent, than the person who just seems to "know" more than the others.

BE PEOPLE-ORIENTED. As described in this chapter, intuition is particularly useful when dealing with human issues. Relying more on intuition, you will discover yourself in a "comfort zone" with people, interacting more honestly and effectively than ever before.

BE ENERGETIC. Intuition will guide you toward sources of positive energy and away from sources of negative energy that dilute your overall effectiveness.

BE CURIOUS. Those with the most developed intuitions know that they are fueled by knowledge and experience. They are acutely inquisitive and driven to learn.

BE COURAGEOUS. Most of the time, the tough calls and tough tasks are tough because the data is not clear and convincing. The left brain cannot arrive at a decision. The intuitive leader allows his or her intuition to "tip the scales."

BE SUPPORTIVE. With its particular strength in dealing with human issues, intuition enables you to build an environment that encourages risk taking, collaboration, self-leadership, and recognition.

GENERATE IDEAS. Left-brain thinking is focused on the known and proven. Right-brain intuition provides the fuel for becoming a thought leader, identifying new associations and connections, and originating new or alternative concepts, approaches, processes, and objectives.

BUILD A PLAN. You will know in your gut the optimal path connecting your vision to results.

ENGAGE A TEAM. Intuition will provide you with the ability to recruit, engage, and inspire the right people to help your organization realize your vision.

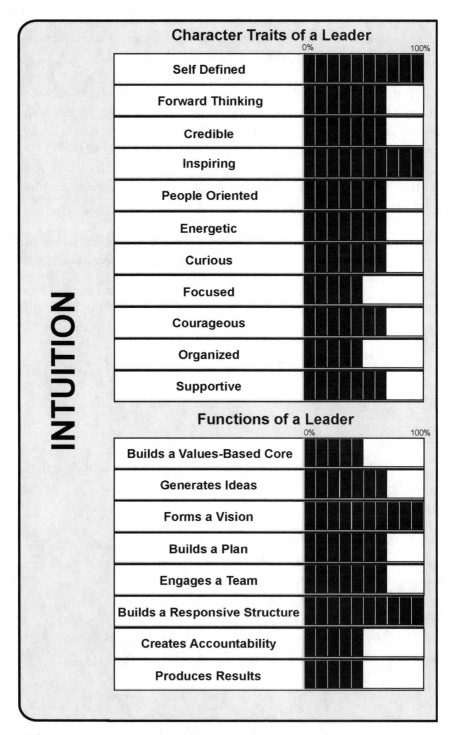

FIGURE 6.1

CHAPTER 7

CREATIVITY
The Seventh Driver of the
High-Impact Leader

I suggested in chapter 1 that energy is a vibration that exists within every person and every tangible and intangible thing, thus linking all things and persons in one whole system. We are inextricably connected with each other and everything in life. Nothing is separate and nothing is independent.

Creativity is the ability to discover, out of the openness discussed in chapter 2, the connections in our lives. To create is to cause to come into being, but what is brought into being in the creative process is not a new element in our existence, but rather the identification of connections between elements that already exist. This is a critical distinction that takes a tremendous amount of pressure out of the creative process. To be creative, you don't have to build something new that never existed before. You simply have to be more aware and see connections that haven't been seen before. You don't have to force any-thing; you only have to allow it to happen.

> *Creativity* **is the ability to discover the connections in our lives.**

Creativity is a key element of *innovation*, which is the commercialization of creativity. If any single feature defines organizations in the twenty-first century, thus far anyway, it is likely the need for innovation. Regardless of the arena, an organization must innovate just to survive, let alone thrive. Every organization—corporate, nonprofit, government, military, sports franchise—will lose out to competitors who are more innovative.

This chapter discusses the dimensions of creativity, ways to enhance your own personal creativity, and how creativity is a key driver of the high-impact leader's ability to be inspiring and energetic, and to generate ideas and form an organizational vision.

CREATIVITY IS LIFE

At the extreme, creativity is binary. We create and we live, or we don't create and we die. Nearly everyone has enough creativity to at least survive, but I believe our level of *prosperity*—our unique, ideal combination of contentment and wealth—depends upon our level of creativity. The more creative we are, the more prosperous we are and the more positive energy we receive out of life. The less creative we are, the less prosperous we are and the less positive energy we receive. One road is toward life. The other is toward inertia, which leads to decay, which leads to death.

Creativity is the essence of our existence. We came into this life through creativity, as our parents identified a connection between themselves and the possibility that might exist if they put their cells together. We survive by identifying just enough connections to put food in our stomachs and shelter us from the elements. We thrive by maximizing the number of connections we see.

CREATIVITY IS A CHOICE

As the natural order of life, creativity lies within every person. Every person is a powerful creative force. It is simply a matter of choice: Do you want to be open to seeing new connections? Do you want to fully engage the creative power of life and channel that power in and through your personal and professional life? In essence, do you want to channel the energy of the universe? Over the past few years, since discovering my own creativity, I have heard hundreds of people, including scores of leaders, say, "I'm not very creative." I tell them, "That's like saying the sun did not come up today. It's a denial of 'what is.' By definition as a human with six senses—taste, touch, hearing, sight, smell, and intuition—you are creative. You are simply not recognizing or exercising it."

As I mentioned in chapter 3, I didn't consider myself creative for most of my adult life. A number of years ago, however, I simply made a choice to be creative. Inspired by my wife, who is highly creative, supportive, and concedes no limits to human potential, I just decided that, in fact, I am really quite creative. A close friend of mine, who is a gifted creator in many media and arenas, dragged me to an art store, bought me the basics to start painting, and demanded I do so. I started painting large abstracts on canvas and, within a year, was selling my paintings for several thousand dollars each. I macraméd hemp bracelets and anklets for myself and everyone I knew who would wear them. I started taking more photographs. I started journaling to myself, and then started writing for others. I wrote a wine column in a Sonoma Valley newspaper for five years. I started writing this book.

In everything I was doing that was not "artistic" in the traditional sense—coaching executives, strategizing for companies, teaching leadership, and forming new companies—I quickly transformed into something creative. As my creativity flourished, so did my relationships. I was less fixed. Seeing more connections, I was less married to any one point of view in particular.

CREATIVITY IS THE HIGH-IMPACT LEADER'S ONLY CHOICE

The high velocity, highly complex nature of the world today demands that organizations, indeed institutions, innovate in order to survive. They must either commercialize creativity or the purpose of their organization will be better served by another organization that is more creative and commercializes its creativity better.

An organization can only be creative, I believe, if its leader is creative. This doesn't necessarily mean creative in a research and development sense, but creative in embodying the traditional traits and functions expected of a leader—that is, creative in leading. Given how technology has leveled the playing field between leaders and their team members, an effective leader today needs to be more creative—to see more connections and have a clearer view of "what is"—than his or her team members, or he or she is irrelevant. We don't need a leader to help us stand still. We need a leader who sees better than us and thus deserves to walk in front of us.

THE DRIVERS OF CREATIVITY

Creativity is driven by the first six personal drivers described earlier in this book. They dramatically enhance our ability to see new connections in the world around us.

PRESENCE. By now, I'm sure I sound like a broken record, but the practice of presence is the most important factor in the development of your creativity. Specifically, meditation (see chapter 1) practiced twice a day for twenty minutes powerfully increases your awareness of the connections in your life.

OPENNESS. Openness (see chapter 2) is the willingness to consider every element of "what is." It removes all that blocks your vision of connections. With visual blocks removed, you begin to see the connections to which most others are blind.

CLARITY. Clarity of thought, emotion, and behavior—in essence, freedom from fear-based thoughts, emotions, and behaviors, such as anger, rage, shame, envy, sadness, and guilt—results in clarity of vision, which results in your ability to identify new connections.

Some people believe an environment of constraint or urgency— perhaps based on time, money, or competition—is favorable for creativity.

That may be true of innovation, but in my experience it is not true of creativity. I agree with Julia Cameron (1992) that creativity develops best in a nurturing environment of love, devoid of constraint and urgency, which are antitheses of clarity of thought, emotion, and behavior. Sometimes you have no choice, but I suggest that when you do, don't press. Let things come and go as they may. I am convinced that the less you press, the heavier the flow of newfound connections.

> To be creative, you don't have to build something new that never existed before. You simply have to be more aware and see connections that haven't been seen before.

INTENTION. Intention, the desire for a result, drives creativity as it does every other result. Intention embodied in practice transforms the possibility of creativity into a certainty. For example, once I decided I wanted to be a painter, I simply willed it into a reality. I bought the materials, created the time in my schedule, and I started painting. I studied, I talked to other artists, I experimented, I made mistakes, and ended up creating saleable work.

PERSONAL RESPONSIBILITY. Personal responsibility, the complete ownership of "what is," means that your basic creative nature cannot be neglected, and your creativity cannot be abdicated.

INTUITION. Intuition, your sixth sense, allows you to identify and understand connections to which you might be blind, or by which you might be confused, if you relied only upon your other five senses.

EXERCISE:
SEE NEW CONNECTIONS

This exercise is really more of a program for developing your creativity—your ability to identify new connections in your existence. The exercises in chapter 2 primed you for creativity. Figuratively speaking, they opened your eyelids; they unblocked your vision. This exercise improves your vision and your ability to make sense out of what you see. Your improved ability to spot connections will dramatically enhance your ability to inspire your team, be highly energetic, generate ideas, and form a vision for your organization.

STEP 1: JOURNAL WITHOUT A PURPOSE

Julia Cameron, author of *The Artist's Way* (1992), a cult favorite among artists and, increasingly, those who don't yet consider themselves artists and are merely seeking ways to develop their creativity, suggests journaling three pages each morning about anything. Inspired by my wife's regular journaling practice, I started this several years ago and the results were profound. There is some magic in just expressing your thoughts to yourself in the present moment. The best way I can explain it is that thinking that stays in your mind or is verbally expressed stays on well-worn tracks passing through familiar territory, while thinking that is expressed in writing jumps the tracks and takes you to new places.

Again, your writing can be about anything whatsoever. In fact, the objective is to allow your mind to wander aimlessly, as deep, far, and wide as your inspiration takes you. There are no rules.

STEP 2: CONNECT THE DOTS

First, jot down random things. For instance, your fingernail and a giant oak tree. Your angst about your high school reunion and the World Series. A stapler and the U.S. Speaker of the House. A cat in Nigeria and a doornail in Moscow. Then add things to the mix. An airplane, a snail, a plastic cup, and a laptop computer. Then, write down all the possible connections between the random things you came up with.

Here's an example: My fingernail and a giant oak tree? Sure! How about they each grow? They each ultimately require oxygen and sunlight. They each shed waste. They each provide protection. They are each quite hardy and require minimal care for survival. Fungus, however, can attack each. Each can crack and break. The nail can scratch the tree. The tree can splinter under the nail. The nail, as a part of the planter's hand, contributes to the planting of the tree. Another thing named "nail" is often pounded into trees. And on and on.

Second, open a book to a random page, read a brief passage, and analyze its possible significance to your life. I first learned a variation of this practice almost thirty years ago in *Illusions*, the classic tale by Richard Bach (1977). The protagonist, Don Shimoda, advises you to open a book, any book, and you'll find the solution to whatever problem you're holding in your mind. I've used this countless times and the results are profound. I remember when I was considering whether I should leave the perceived safety of Citicorp to take a position with a then-up-and-coming investment bank, Montgomery Securities. I was very perplexed by the choice I had to make. I opened a book written by Peter Drucker, the late, great management guru, and the page in front of me described how three men in the late 1950s left their established firms on Wall Street and formed Donaldson, Lufkin & Jenrette, which went on to become a major investment bank. I knew right then what my decision would and must be, and I have never regretted it.

These two actions—jotting down random things and making connections, and opening a book randomly and analyzing its significance to your life now—are designed to help you see connections everywhere you can. If you don't see them, it only means you don't recognize them. They are there. Nothing is random. Practice these as often as you can, every day if possible, and you will see your creative side begin to flourish.

STEP 3: ENGAGE IN AN ART

Engage in an artistic pursuit for at least four hours each week. Learn a new musical instrument. Write an article or a novel. Learn ceramics. Carve wood. Build a piece of furniture. Learn to dance. Join a community acting troupe. Knit a scarf. Quilt. Do anything, provided it is outside of your comfort zone.

I mentioned earlier that I started painting as my first artistic pursuit and the effects were immediate and amazing. As a result, I quickly became more creative in all aspects of my personal and professional life. And I found myself more content in all aspects as well.

As I discussed above, many leaders believe they are not creative, which is a denial of the basic nature of life. Many others believe they are creative, but consider any expression of it an extravagant luxury to which they are not entitled in their busy, time-constrained, obligation-ridden existence. This mind-set is as harmful as the first. The reality is that creative expression is as important as any activity that now fills up your time. Because our contemporary world demands creativity from you and your organization, you cannot afford to ignore your creativity. You must make the development of creativity among your highest priorities.

STEP 4: FEED YOUR BRAIN

Feed, feed, feed your brain. The best way to feed is to read, read, read. Read everything you can get your hands on: classic and contemporary novels, biographies, history, science, science fiction, self-help, trade journals in and outside of your trade, pop-culture magazines, mainstream newspapers, alternative newspapers. And beyond reading, listen to books on tape, watch movies, listen to talk radio, talk to as many diverse people as you can, attend lectures and seminars, surf the Internet, travel into new areas.

I am still amazed at the number of leaders who don't feed their brain. Not coincidentally, they are not very creative, and they are not high-impact leaders. They say, "I don't have time." I say, "You don't have time not to feed your brain, because someone else who wants your customers or your team members is feeding his or her brain, identifying new connections, and discovering new ways to serve them better than you are."

STEP 5: PLAY IN A NEW FIELD

Step outside of your field and become a novice in a new field—and then another field, then another, for the rest of your life.

For example, if you are a business executive without a background in electrical engineering, start learning electrical engineering. If you are the leader of a social services organization, start learning law. If you are a leader of a sports franchise, start learning Chinese medicine. I'm not suggesting sacrificing your current career. Far from it. Instead, I suggest that you enhance your current career by becoming dramatically more creative and by seeing new connections to which you would otherwise be blind. These new connections will enhance your leadership.

The business executive will start to see connections between electrical engineering and her business. The social services leader will start to see connections between law and his organization. The sports franchise leader will see connections between Chinese medicine and her team and sport. These connections will improve their leadership and organizations. If you look around, you'll see that much creativity today is the result of people playing in a new field. For example, quantum computing, the likely future of computing, resulted from electrical engineers playing in the field of quantum science.

Once most people leave academia and embark upon their careers, they immerse themselves in a field and don't stray too far. By immersion, I mean going deep into a subject or environment to the relative exclusion of other subjects or environments. Lawyers immerse themselves in law, engineers in engineering, doctors in medicine, bankers in finance, businesspeople in business, and so on. Historically, of course, there has been an economic incentive to immerse. You immersed yourself, you became highly skilled, and you were paid well for your expertise.

Today an economic incentive to go deep into a subject or environment still exists, but there is a cost to excluding others. Immersion blinds you to all the connections outside your area of expertise as well as the connections from outside your area to your area. In fact, in one sense, *expertise*—applying knowledge in a highly competent manner—is really the antithesis of creativity because it involves the known. To be a high-impact leader, you must continuously make new connections—within your field and especially outside of it. Google, creator of the world's leading Internet search engine and *Fortune* magazine's 2007 selection as the best company to work for in the United States, clearly agrees. With its requirement that engineers spend 20 percent of their time on their own self-defined projects, it is one of the leaders in recognizing that tomorrow's definition of expertise and, more importantly, the creation of value involves exploring beyond the known (Lashinsky 2007, 79).

STEP 6: TRAVEL TO A NEW FIELD

Travel to new lands and explore new cultures. Just as many of us become immersed in our careers, many of us are also "locationally" immersed. We don't play in enough fields around the world. We miss out on all the connections that might be drawn between foreign lands and cultures and our own lives. Yvon Chouinard, the founder and leader of Patagonia, the highly innovative and very successful apparel and outdoor gear company, credits much of his leadership success to his and his team members' practice of getting outside, traveling, and having new experiences (Chouinard 2005, 168–86).

I have found it helpful to be more conscious about my travel choices. Like most other leaders, I do not have an abundance of available travel time, so I try to ensure that my travels themselves are abundant in newness and diversity.

STEP 7: PARTNER UP

Enlist several partners with whom you can talk creatively. Find people who share your interest in developing their own creativity, and then spend thirty minutes or so every few weeks with them to brainstorm without agenda or limits.

Over the past several years, I have built a small network of people around the country with whom I talk on a regular basis about business- and leadership-related ideas as far-ranging as you can imagine. I receive several benefits from this exercise: it is extremely enjoyable, it builds intimate relationships (most of us can use more of those), and, most relevant to this discussion, it is a powerful enabler of creativity.

The High-Impact Leader Empowered by Creativity: George Hsu

George Hsu is a brilliant, Stanford-educated engineer. From early in his career, and likely his life, he was open to possibilities. As a result of his openness, he saw things others did not. In his senior year at Stanford, one of his professors stated that no significant innovation had been made in compassing technology in many decades. The professor challenged his students to design a digital electromagnetic compass—something that had never been done before. In a matter of several weeks, George had designed and filed a patent on the world's first digital compass, and upon his graduation he formed a company to develop electromagnetic and other sensor-based products. The company now generates nearly $20 million in annual revenue.

But George's success didn't stop there. For years, as he developed an increasing number of sensor-based products, he pondered why a new integrated circuit had to be custom-designed and developed for every new product he developed. The process took twelve to twenty-four months and was a major issue when getting a product to market in a timely manner was important, which was most of the time. He queried hundreds of engineers about the possibility of a standard integrated circuit that would process any type of sensor signal—pressure, gas, tilt, moisture, to name only a few. A standard integrated circuit would eliminate the costly custom design and development cycle. Everyone said it couldn't be done. They said the types of signals varied too much in their physical properties and it was impossible to normalize them in a single chip.

George, however, was open to the possibility that it could be done. So he set about doing it. After a couple of years of work, he completed a design that did exactly what he wanted and what everyone else said could not be done. He raised venture capital and started a new company, Sensor Platforms, to produce the chip for companies developing sensor-based applications. He quickly got the attention of a number of potential major customers, and he now plans to sell hundreds of millions of these parts within just a few years.

George believes strongly that the mind must be "cross-trained" constantly to enable one to spot connections that escape the attention of others. Thus, George is constantly seeking "dots" to connect. He engages in as many different activities and interests as time will allow. Professionally, he studies mechanical, structural, and chemical engineering, seeking insights that might facilitate his creativity in electrical engineering. He is an outstanding tennis player. An excellent trombonist, he recently began taking voice lessons. He listens to many types of music, from classical to hip-hop. In addition to English, he speaks Mandarin Chinese and German, and is studying French. He is a serious reader across diverse topics. And he networks extremely well, with a diverse set of friends and acquaintances all over the world.

Creativity is a key element of George's success as a leader. Lacking creativity, other leaders may see rocks in their paths as brick walls. George analogizes the creative leader to water in a stream, impervious to whatever lies in its path, always moving forward, never stopping. There is always a connection from where the stream is now to where it wants to go, revealing itself on a just-in-time basis. The creative leader does not stall.

George's team members find his creativity inspirational. Fed by his many interests, he exudes energy and optimism in everything he does. He is a font of ideas, always the thought leader. Fearless, he envisions futures that others can't see and then makes them happen.

THE LEADERSHIP DASHBOARD

Figure 7.1, the Leadership Dashboard, demonstrates graphically how creativity is a key source of energy empowering you as a leader to embody many of the character traits, and perform many of the functions, of the high-impact leader that were described in the introduction. It shows that creativity, fueled itself by the drivers of presence and openness, enables you to:

BE INSPIRING. Creativity, the ability to discover new connections, allows you to identify the common purpose in your organization, and then articulate your vision in a way that your team members see themselves integrally involved in it.

BE ENERGETIC. Creativity is one of the fundamental energies of life. Unlike inertia, which depletes life energy, creativity is restorative, regenerative, and invigorating.

GENERATE IDEAS. You will be a thought leader, identifying new associations and connections, and originating new ways of thinking and doing things.

FORM A VISION. Unbounded by fear, flowing with ideas, and thinking forward, you'll be highly effective at formulating optimal, achievable, and valuable organizational objectives.

The driver of creativity will also fuel your ability to:

BE FORWARD THINKING. The creative mind, acutely aware of connections everywhere, sees infinite possibilities.

BE CREDIBLE. In an existence where organizational survival depends upon innovating, or commercializing creativity, you must be highly creative to establish and maintain your team members' confidence in you as their leader who sees more connections and possibilities and is best positioned to lead them to a better future.

BE CURIOUS. The creative mind becomes addicted to new connections and never ceases to inquire.

BE COURAGEOUS. Being able to see more leads to understanding more, which leads to fearing less. You will find yourself more able than ever to make the tough calls, perform the tough tasks, and take the risks that should be taken.

BE ORGANIZED. Your creativity will enable you to coordinate and direct activities in a functional, structured whole.

BUILD A PLAN. In your creativity, you will see the connections forming the optimal path leading from vision to results.

ENGAGE A TEAM. With the level playing field today, where information is available to all, it is your creativity—your ability to see more connections and have a clearer view of "what is" out of all that information—that will attract team members to your team.

BUILD A RESPONSIVE STRUCTURE. Your creativity will allow you to envision the optimal structure for success in our high velocity, highly complex environment.

PRODUCE RESULTS. Creativity allows you to achieve your vision in the most efficient, holistic, and measurable manner.

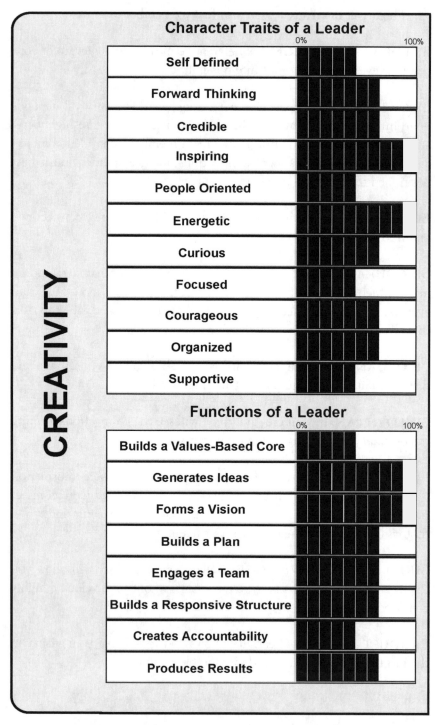

FIGURE 7.1

CHAPTER 8

CONNECTED COMMUNICATION
The Eighth Driver of the High-Impact Leader

Today we communicate constantly via in-person dialogue, e-mail, text messages, instant messages, mobile phones, and landline phones. We receive nearly nonstop communication via television, radio, the Internet, newspapers, magazines, and advertising media.

But when I ask people about communication today, the overwhelming majority of them tell me that their relationships have not improved with the rapid increase in modes of communication. In fact, most decry the quality of their relationships with family members, friends, and professional colleagues. They tell me they want to go "deeper" and have more meaningful exchanges; they want interactions that strengthen relationships and build contentment.

Given that the amount of communication is increasing but the quality of our relationships is decreasing, the quality of our communication must in some way be deficient. We "talk a lot, but don't improve our lot." To improve our lot, to be more content, to live more effectively, to lead more effectively, I believe we have to improve the quality of our communication. We have to communicate in a far more connected way.

Connected communication is an exchange between two or more people, facilitated by empathy, honesty, and clarity of purpose and message.

In this chapter, you'll see how connected communication is more than a leadership tool or mechanical practice. It is an intensely powerful driver that lies deep within the high-impact leader. When using connected communication, the high-impact leader is present, mindful, and completely honest. He or she is clear and concise, acutely empathic, and completely in touch with "what is." Everyone around the high-impact leader senses the integrity, the wholeness, of who he or she is and how he or she communicates, and gathers strength in his or her presence.

This chapter explains the system of connected communication, from clear expression of a purposeful message by an empathic speaker to an empathic listener, and it provides tools for optimizing the process. It shows how clear communication lies beneath the high-impact leader's ability to be inspiring and supportive as well as to engage a team and create accountability.

SPEAKER-LISTENER, LISTENER-SPEAKER

In this chapter, I will refer to the *speaker* as a person who expresses thought or emotion through the spoken or written word, nonverbal communication, or even silence. I'll refer to the speaker's expression as his or her *voice*. The *listener* is the person on the receiving end of the voice, and his or her perception of the speaker's expression is his or her *ear*.

Three elements, however, complicate matters. First, in most communications, we actually perform the roles of speaker and listener simultaneously. When we speak, for instance, we both communicate our message and "listen" for how it is being perceived. When we listen, we both perceive the speaker's message and "speak" our response to it. Second, in a *dialogue*—a communication between two or more people—we constantly switch roles. The speaker with the voice becomes the listener with the ear, and vice versa, and over and over again. Third, any communication affects more people than just the speaker and the listener. In the simplest of communications, you tell your spouse something that a friend said to you. That communication now involves two listeners, you and your spouse. As a chief executive, you might convey something to your senior managers that your board of directors said to you. That communication now involves multiple speakers and listeners. The larger the speaker's platform, the greater the number of people the communication will affect. For example, the utterances of the chief executive of a major corporation potentially affect many more lives than those of an owner of a small retail shop.

Because of this interactive, dynamic quality of communication, I avoid compartmentalizing and simplifying the critical components of connected communication into speaking and listening. The functions are too interconnected for that. Thus, I suggest that each component discussed below will enhance both speaking and listening to varying degrees, depending upon the situation. For instance, presence and empathy apply equally to speaking and listening. Persuasion applies more to speaking, while message acknowledgment, as its name implies, applies more to listening. All of this will become clearer as we delve into the qualities of connected communication below.

BE PRESENT

As I have discussed, the driver of presence underlies each of the other seven drivers of the high-impact leader, including the driver of connected communication. The practice of meditation (see chapter 1) is a powerful tool for grounding yourself, becoming highly aware of your needs and desires, and knowing how best to communicate those needs and desires. Meditation also helps you increase your awareness of the needs of others.

Presence, of course, involves only "what is." Anything other than "what is" in the present moment is not real. For a speaker, then, connected communication allows for nothing but complete honesty. Connected communication involves no deception, manipulation, or exaggeration.

> *Connected communication* is an exchange between two or more people, facilitated by empathy, honesty, and clarity of purpose and message.

For a listener, connected communication means listening for content, for a complete understanding of the message and the feelings of the speaker in the present moment. This explicitly excludes what might be called "pseudo-listening," which is not really listening at all. Pseudo-listening includes practices such as focusing on form over content, faking listening as you look for a break to interrupt the speaker, daydreaming about other things, or formulating your response.

GET INTO THE SHOES OF THE OTHER

Empathy empowers us to realize the true interconnected nature of life and to connect with others in a meaningful, fulfilling way. It is the essence, the linchpin, of connected communication. Without empathy, communication lacks connection. Communication without the connection is at best mundane and unfulfilling and at worst, dangerous and life threatening.

Empathy is one of the most powerful practices in which you will ever engage. According to Arthur Ciaramicoli and Katherine Ketcham, authors of *The Power of Empathy*, being empathic means

> we are capable of understanding each other on a deep level, actually feeling the emotions and understanding the thoughts, ideas, motives, and judgments of others. Empathy is the bond that connects us, helping us to think before we act, motivating us to reach out to someone in pain, teaching us to use our reasoning powers to balance our emotions and inspiring us to the most lofty ideals to which human beings can aspire (Ciaramicoli and Ketcham 2001, 10).

Empathy is necessary at each end of the communication process. It is as important to the optimization of speaking as it is to the optimization of listening. At least conceptually, it is easy to achieve. You simply attempt to answer the following questions about the people with whom you communicate: Who are you? What do you believe? What and whom do you love? What and whom do you fear? What do you desire?

Given the protective shell under which many people live and take comfort, you generally won't ask these questions outright, although I find myself doing that more and more when I sense an openness in the person with whom I'm speaking. Rather, you'll usually attempt to learn as much as you can under the circumstances before engaging deeply in the communication. "Under the circumstances" generally means that the more important the communication is or potentially could be to you, and the more time you have available, the more time you will invest in the learning process. Thus, the process sometimes occurs in a few moments, and at other times occurs over hours or days.

ACKNOWLEDGE, ACKNOWLEDGE, ACKNOWLEDGE

Sometimes I think acknowledgment may be the solution to all of the world's conflicts. As a young trial attorney many years ago in Alaska, I volunteered as a mediator at a conflict resolution center in the community. The key to a successful mediation, in case after case, was acknowledgment. I found that parties in conflict wanted nothing, including money and property, more than acknowledgment. When parties received acknowledgment from me, the dispute could usually be settled about half the time. When the parties acknowledged each other, I never had a case that did not settle.

Two powerful types of acknowledgment are critical to connected communication. You use the first, *feelings acknowledgment*, when you communicate that you understand the feelings of the other. While empathy provides you with an understanding of the feelings of the other person, this type of acknowledgment closes the loop and communicates that understanding to that person. This is a tool for both speakers and listeners. Given the concept discussed in chapter 1 that there is an equal and opposite reaction to every action, when you acknowledge the other's feelings, it almost guarantees that he or she will seek to understand your feelings. Just start asking other people how they feel and you'll be amazed at how they start asking you the same.

You use the second, *message acknowledgment*, when you as a listener understand the message of the other. It involves questioning the speaker

177

> **Connected communication involves no deception, manipulation, or exaggeration.**

and then summarizing the speaker's message to ensure the accuracy and meaning of what was perceived. Often referred to as "active listening," this type of acknowledgment is powerful because it communicates to the speaker that his or her message is important. When the speaker is acknowledged in this way, he or she is more likely to seek to understand your message.

The effect of each type of acknowledgment is profound. Just think about the times you have been acknowledged in a sincere way by someone whom you respect. It was probably immensely gratifying and made you very open to the other things that person was communicating to you.

DETERMINE YOUR PURPOSE AND FORM YOUR STRATEGY

Every communication has a purpose or multiple purposes. Even when you don't think you have a purpose, you actually do. Sometimes it's just entertainment. Often, it is a desire to learn. You will find it immensely helpful at the beginning of any communication to do a quick mental check of your purpose. Are you trying to persuade? Are you trying to inform? Are you trying to learn? Are you socializing? Or are you venting?

I then suggest forming a strategy to accomplish your purpose. In my experience, this is something very few people do, or at least very few people do well. They have a sense about the purpose of the communication, but they spend little time and energy in developing a strategy for accomplishing it. Ask yourself, what will define a successful communication? What do I need to do to achieve that result?

PERSUADING

Persuading involves trying to convince one or more people of something. At a structural level, Yale University psychologist William McGuire

(1969, 3:173) broke the process of persuasion down into five key steps. Each step must be satisfied, or the persuasion process stalls and fails:

1. The speaker must win the attention of the listener, which is best done by creating a message that appeals to the listener.

2. The speaker must assist the listener in comprehending the message. Clear language and vivid examples are very helpful.

3. The speaker must secure belief from the listener. If the speaker has preexisting credibility with the listener, this step is much easier. Without preexisting credibility, the speaker usually relies upon evidence that supports his or her message, as well as sincere enthusiasm about the message.

4. The speaker must ensure that the listener retains the message, which is best accomplished by repeating the message several times. Obviously, the best speakers are extraordinarily talented at using memorable catch-phrases or catchwords that simply do not allow the listener to forget the message.

5. The speaker must request clear and prompt action.

Many years ago, one of my former partners at Montgomery Securities, John Skeen, gave me a practical approach to this process. He pulled me aside after my first presentation to the partners. He said, "David, that was okay, but remember that every element—indeed every word—of every persuasive communication you ever make in a business setting must meet the following three criteria, or it must be thrown out: it must be focused, conclusive, and engender greed or fear. There is no time to be anything but on point. No one wants your details; just provide your conclusions. And embed the message with something that tugs on the basic needs of your listener." To this day, I edit my business communications accordingly.

INFORMING

While conveying information, self-confidence and confidence in your message, discernible to the listener, are critical in establishing your credibility. The key is to deliver your message with confidence but without condescension, arrogance, or closed-mindedness. If you are truly "in the shoes" of the other, this shouldn't be an issue. Your mission then is to convey information clearly and concisely.

LEARNING

In trying to extract information from the other, there are two primary considerations that affect strategy: the quantity of information you need or want, and the time and other needs of the other.

If the amount of information is large, you might use open-ended questions, allow the other to deliver the information as he or she sees best, and fill in the voids with more specific questions later. If the information is small, you might be very direct and specific.

You'll want to respect the time needs of the other. Look for signals from him or her, and consider asking directly, about the time he or she has available for you and make adjustments accordingly. What about his or her other needs? Do your best to anticipate possible fears and make his or her communication with you as safe as is possible. If the other needs confidentiality, then commit to it if you are able and honor it without exception, or explain why you cannot commit to it.

Above and beyond the time needs and fears of the other, consider the exchange needed by the other. If you consider that nothing in life is a one-way flow, then you must consider what the person producing the information needs in exchange. Given that this is usually an implied need, intuition is critical in identifying it. Perhaps the other needs the feeling that you will offer information he or she needs back to him or her at some point in the future. Perhaps he or she needs your gratitude. Perhaps he or she needs your respect or approval.

SOCIALIZING

Here you are just communicating for enjoyment or to build a relationship. There usually is not a lot of strategy needed for social communication. The purpose is being social, so the strategy is generally to have fun, communicate love, or share experiences, thoughts, and emotions. I have found it is useful, however, to examine my social interactions for ways I can improve them.

VENTING

In these communications, you "air out" your emotions. You might be angry, for instance, and need to express your anger to another person to relieve the tension inside of you.

Unlike socializing, a lot more strategy could be used here. In my experience, most people vent too frequently and with too little forethought. They then come across as negative people and often alienate more positive-minded people with whom they interact.

I suggest four rules for venting:

1. Remember the old maxim of questionable origination, "Never attribute to malice what can be adequately explained by ignorance or stupidity."

    Our fears tend to take us immediately to the place of believing that someone has a mission to damage us. In reality, that is rarely the case. People just don't have time to intentionally wreck our lives. But we ascribe the worst to the other and then react with the malice we have perceived on his or her part.

2. Let some time pass. By definition, venting is reacting, but you likely want to reduce the amount of venom in the reaction and time usually helps greatly. The amount of time varies, but it must be enough so that the next rule can be satisfied.

3. Express what you feel and only what you feel—not how wrong someone is or what a jerk someone is. A person who was neglected at an important company meeting might be initially inclined to react with the following comment to his friend: "Joe, my manager, is an &#*@!&!!!! He's as bad as they come. What a jerk! I wish they'd fire his &#*!!!" A much healthier reaction would be: "I feel angry that Joe did not ask my opinion at the meeting. I feel hurt. I am afraid that he may not think highly enough of my opinions to ask me about them in front of a group of people. That makes me sad, and I am afraid that I may not have a future with this company as long as Joe is my manager."

4. After expressing your emotions, focus the communication on the positive things you can do to improve the situation. The neglected employee might say to his friend, "I am thinking about asking Joe to grab a cup of coffee with me and expressing how I feel. What would you suggest?"

BE SELF-CONFIDENT AND POSITIVE

Self-confidence discernible to the other is critical to establishing your credibility and the credibility of your purpose. Interestingly, as a persuasive speaker, discernible confidence in the message is not always necessary. I used to do a lot of business with a corporate securities lawyer who was a master at dropping a suggested solution almost apologetically into a roomful of twenty-five highly opinionated, powerful business executives, investment bankers, accountants, and other lawyers, and watching the suggestion sprout over time into the group consensus. Reminding me of the character played by Peter Falk in the old television series *Columbo*, he would frame it something like, "Hmmm, this is a tough issue. It just struck me, and I know this is probably crazy, probably makes no sense at all, but what if we structured this deal as a license agreement instead of an outright sale? I don't know, probably a really stupid idea, but just thought I'd throw it out."

He was brilliant in two ways. First, he seemed to always have the best solution to any problem that arose. Second, he knew how to sell it to a tough audience. The audience had too much ego to have an opinion crammed down its throat. But it was smart enough to identify the best solution once it was articulated. Invariably, after several hours, the lawyer's "stupid idea" had been adopted by the group and, amazingly, each person at the table thought he or she was a major contributor to reaching the solution. Clearly, the lawyer's seeming lack of confidence in the message did not hurt him; rather, it helped him immensely. But his self-confidence was evident to the discerning in a couple ways. First, he was secure enough with himself that he could label his idea as "stupid," thus deprecating himself in front of a tough crowd. He didn't worry about being labeled stupid along with the idea. Second, he had so much confidence in the idea itself that he could "soft sell" it.

A positive attitude and absence of negative emotion are also important for establishing and maintaining your credibility and your ability to engage a listener. It sounds so obvious and yet is ignored so often. Most of us have experienced the leader who starts off a staff meeting with "I've reviewed the performance report from last week and I'm not happy. I don't know what the hell is going on and I'm going to find out right now. Don't plan on getting out of here early today, because you have a lot of explaining to do." Contrast that with the leader who says, "Thank you for your efforts to date. I know how hard you are working to make us the best in our class. We have some challenges, however, and I want to explain them to you and work with you to build a plan to overcome them." Which leader would you rather have? Which leader will bring out the best in you?

ENGAGE THE LISTENER

By definition, a speaker is engaged because he or she is actively involved in speaking. This section, therefore, addresses the speaker's challenge of engaging the listener. An engaged listener perceives the speaker's message and is responsive to the speaker's purpose. The listener doesn't necessarily agree with the purpose, or won't necessarily cooperate with accomplishing the speaker's purpose, but he or she understands the purpose and is responsive to it, either positively or negatively.

With empathy—the ability to say, "I know who you are, what you believe, what and who you love, what and who you fear, and what you desire," or at least a start on that—the speaker is well prepared to engage the listener. The listener appreciates the speaker's personal acknowledgment and naturally wants to offer exchange. The exchange, of course, is engaging in the communication with the speaker, and listening to what he or she has to say.

As the communication develops, you as the speaker can consider two practices to build engagement. First, you can share of yourself. This naturally inspires the listener to share of himself or herself. The listener is then further invested in the process, beyond just the time spent in the communication, and more inclined to engage. Second, you can solicit questions and feedback. The questions give you an opportunity to overcome objections or other barriers to accomplishment of your purpose, and allow you to get deeper "in the shoes" of the listener and modify your strategy if necessary.

LISTEN TO YOURSELF

Interestingly, at least with the verbal voice, listening to ourselves is one of the most neglected practices in communication. With the written voice, we usually listen to ourselves by editing what we write before we communicate our message. With our verbal voice, few of us rehearse and once it has been expressed, we usually don't pay close attention to exactly how it sounded. Interestingly, most people I know who listen to recordings of themselves are unhappy with the way they sound.

I have found it highly beneficial to record myself in practice communications. If I have an important telephone call to make, meeting to attend, or speech to deliver, I'll do more than just jot an outline of what I'd like to convey. I'll record my comments on a little digital recorder ahead of time and then listen carefully for ways that I can improve. Alternatively, I'll rehearse what I want to say in front of someone whom I can trust for candid constructive criticism.

CAREFULLY CRAFT AND SCRUTINIZE THE MESSAGE

With every communication, you as speaker should ask yourself, "What message will open my listener to my purpose and elicit the response I would like?" As the communication develops, another good question is, "How is my listener responding to my message?"

As a listener, you should try to ask yourself in every communication, "What is the speaker's purpose and message?" As the communication unfolds, you might ask, "What response do I want to convey to the speaker?"

Ideally, the messages exchanged are crystal clear, perfectly reflective of what the parties intended to communicate. To attain the ideal—a connected communication—words, silences, and nonverbal messages must be carefully crafted by the speaker and highly scrutinized by the listener to maintain connected communication.

WORDS. As a speaker, your first task is to choose your words very carefully. Use the words, the phrasing, and the intonation that will work for your communication purpose, not for your comfort, convenience, or ego.

As a listener, careful attention must be paid to the words used by the speaker. If the speaker is inarticulate, however, you'll have to work through his or her words to perceive the message being communicated. A former investment banking client of mine, for example, could never say anything clearly. When he gave me the assignment to sell his company, he grumbled something over the telephone like, "Well, I'm not really liking this situation. We'll just stay in close contact and see what happens." I had no idea I had the assignment until I talked to his chief financial officer immediately after. His reference to staying in close contact was tantamount to what most people would express as "You're hired and I look forward to working with you." Over the course of my relationship with him, I learned to look for the message beneath or behind his words, and I became quite competent at it.

SILENCES. Your second task is to choose your silences carefully. As someone once said, the silences in music are as important as the sounds.

185

The same is true in connected communication. If you are trying to persuade or inform the listener of something, slow your "pitch" down to a comfortable cadence so that your listener doesn't feel like he or she is being pressured, has no opportunity to object, or has no voice. If your purpose is to learn, then you won't learn much if you aren't being silent and listening. Silence can be a powerful "vacuum" of information. People are generally uncomfortable with silence and naturally want to fill it. Unfortunately, the silence often invites mundane chatter, but at other times, it inspires the sharing of very valuable information.

I always remember a meeting led by a real estate acquisitions officer with whom I worked many years ago in which he asked the potential seller of a shopping center to tell him all the negative things he should know about the center. The seller rattled off a few obvious things, but the acquisitions officer just sat silently and waited. I was amazed at the amount of valuable information the seller began to reveal. He was clearly uncomfortable with silence and wanted to fill it, even with information that was to his financial detriment. By the end of the hour, the seller had revealed problems—many of which the acquisitions officer could not have discovered by other means—that totaled over a million dollars in value, and he was forced to settle for a far lower price than the acquisitions officer was originally prepared to pay.

NONVERBAL MESSAGES. Your third task is to choose your nonverbal messages carefully. In my experience, the nonverbal messages are as important as the verbal ones. Unfortunately, many of them are either unintended or belie the verbal message. Pay close attention to your facial expressions, hand gestures, eye movement, and body posture. For instance, not looking someone in the eye will often completely undermine your sincerity. You may feel that staring at something in the distance is just a by-product of deliberate and intense thought, but your listener may feel you are being disingenuous. Conversely, staring right into their eyes as you deliver a promise is usually interpreted almost like a contractual seal.

BE BOLD YET SUPPORTIVE

The high-impact leader is a master at being bold yet supportive in his or her communication. He or she communicates the tough calls in the most positive manner possible. The message, even if it has negative consequences for the listener—such as a termination, a demotion, a reassignment, or some other denial, rejection, refusal, or removal of something the listener wants—can be delivered in a supportive way that does not make the listener "wrong." Criticism, of course, is never positive unless it is delivered in an environment of support. Suppression never accomplishes anything positive. Support always does, regardless of the message.

I am continually amazed at the number of leaders who shrink from the task of delivering bad news. For instance, it is almost epidemic how leaders will leave underperforming team members in place because they are afraid of having the tough conversation in which they demote, reassign, or terminate them. The answer, I believe, is first in taking personal responsibility (see chapter 5) and then in learning how to be supportive in his or her communications.

Terminating a team member is one of the most difficult tasks any leader has to face. I can say, however, as someone who has studied and applied the principles of connected communication for over twenty years, that I have only had one or two negative termination experiences in my career. A team member who is not performing up to expectations, and whose performance has not been responsive to remediation efforts, knows that he or she is not a fit for the organization long before the leader delivers the message. I have found in most cases that the actual discussion, provided it occurs in an environment of honesty and support, usually brings great relief and a level of healing to the leader and his or her departing team member.

The High-Impact Leader Empowered by Connected Communication: Martin Luther King Jr.

Like many people, I consider Dr. Martin Luther King Jr. to be one of the greatest leaders in history. Over the course of fifteen years as a political and social activist, Dr. King's organization and leadership of African-Americans' nonviolent quest for the right to vote, desegregation, labor rights, and other basic civil rights resulted in the Civil Rights Act of 1964 and the Voting Rights Act of 1965.

Connected communication was at the heart of his greatness. He was a master of empathy and acknowledgment. He "got into the shoes" of African-Americans everywhere. His speeches, essays, books, and, more importantly, daily interactions with people were characterized by a message along the lines of this: "I feel your pain, humiliation, fear, oppression, and isolation. I feel how the injustices of our society wear on you. And I know what you want. I know you yearn for freedom, acceptance, respect, opportunity, and love."

His communications were highly strategic and extraordinarily well articulated. He had a purpose, and he carefully planned his message and delivery to ensure his purpose was served. He expressed his empathy and acknowledged the feelings of African-Americans with vivid imagery and metaphorical prose. Then he described a better life and used exactly the right words to evoke a commitment from his followers to use peaceful resistance to bring about that better life.

I have read all of Dr. King's books, most of his essays and interviews, as well as most of the books about him. I regularly listen to recordings of his major speeches and am continually inspired by his use of connected communication. I still believe his "I Have a Dream" speech—delivered at the Lincoln Memorial on August 28, 1963, as the keynote address of the March on Washington for Civil Rights—is the most compelling speech, and exemplary use of connected communication, I have ever heard. Given its oft-cited nature, I won't repeat it here. But I will cite Dr. King's concluding comments, transcribed by James Washington, in his sermon at the Mason Temple in Memphis, Tennessee, the night before he was assassinated:

> You know, several years ago, I was in New York City autographing the first book that I had written. And while sitting there autographing books, a demented black woman came up. The only question I heard from her was, "Are you Martin Luther King?"
>
> And I was looking down writing, and I said yes. And the next minute I felt something beating on my chest. Before I knew it I had been stabbed by this demented woman. I was rushed to Harlem Hospital. It was a dark Saturday afternoon. And that blade had gone through, and the X-rays revealed that the tip of the blade was on the edge of my aorta, the main artery. And once that's punctured, you drown in your own blood— that's the end of you.
>
> It came out, in the *New York Times* the next morning, that if I had sneezed, I would have died. Well, about four days later, they allowed me, after the operation, after my chest had been opened, and the blade had been taken out, to move around in the wheel chair in the hospital. They allowed me to read some of the mail that came in, and from all over the states, and the world, kind letters came in. I read a few, but one of them I will never forget. I had received one from the President and the Vice-President. I've forgotten what those telegrams said. I'd received a visit and a letter from the Governor of New York, but I've forgotten what the letter said. But there was another letter that came from a little girl, a young girl who was a student at the White Plains High School. And I looked at that letter, and I'll never forget it. It said simply, "Dear Dr. King: I am a ninth-grade student at the White Plains High School." She said, "While it should not matter, I would like to mention that I am a white girl. I read in the paper of your

misfortune, and of your suffering. And I read that if you had sneezed, you would have died. And I'm simply writing you to say that I'm so happy that you didn't sneeze."

And I want to say tonight, I want to say that I am happy that I didn't sneeze. Because if I had sneezed, I wouldn't have been around here in 1960, when students all over the South started sitting-in at lunch counters. And I knew that as they were sitting in, they were really standing up for the best in the American dream. And taking the whole nation back to those great wells of democracy which were dug deep by the Founding Fathers in the Declaration of Independence and the Constitution. If I had sneezed, I wouldn't have been around in 1962, when Negroes in Albany, Georgia, decided to straighten their backs up. And whenever men and women straighten their backs up, they are going somewhere, because a man can't ride your back unless it is bent. If I had sneezed, I wouldn't have been here in 1963, when the black people of Birmingham, Alabama, aroused the conscience of this nation, and brought into being the Civil Rights Bill. If I had sneezed, I wouldn't have had a chance later that year, in August, to try to tell American [sic] about a dream that I had had. If I had sneezed, I wouldn't have been down in Selma, Alabama, to see the great movement there. If I had sneezed, I wouldn't have been in Memphis to see a community rally around those brothers and sisters who are suffering. I'm so happy that I didn't sneeze.

And they were telling me, now it doesn't matter now. It really doesn't matter what happens now. I left Atlanta this morning, and as we got started on the plane, there were six of us, the pilot said over the public address system, "We are sorry for the delay, but we have Dr. Martin Luther King on the plane. And to be sure that all of the bags were checked, and to be sure that nothing would be wrong with the plane, we had to check out everything carefully. And we've had the plane protected and guarded all night."

And then I got into Memphis. And some began to say the threats, or talk about the threats that were out. What would happen to me from some of our sick white brothers?

Well, I don't know what will happen now. We've got some difficult days ahead. But it doesn't matter with me now. Because I've been to the mountaintop. And I don't mind. Like anybody, I would like to live a long life. Longevity has its place. But I'm not concerned about that now. I just want to do God's will. And He's allowed me to go up to the mountain. And I've looked over. And I've seen the promised land. I may not get there with you. But I want you to know tonight, that we, as a people will get to the promised land. And I'm happy, tonight. I'm not worried about anything. I'm not fearing any man. Mine eyes have seen the glory of the coming of the Lord. (Washington 1986, 285–86)

I cannot listen to a recording of this sermon without my eyes tearing. Sometimes I think my tears are more for the vacuum in which we now exist—tears of loss for the dearth of connected communication among our leaders, and tears of hope for the life we might have in its rediscovery.

THE LEADERSHIP DASHBOARD

The Leadership Dashboard (figure 8.1) shows how the high-impact leader uses the driver of connected communication to optimize certain leadership character traits and functions. It shows on a 100-point scale that connected communication enables you to:

BE INSPIRING. Connected communication, by definition, involves listening deeply to others. Armed with knowledge of and empathy for your team members, you will be able to identify the common purpose binding you to each other and the organization, and able to give life to your vision by communicating it so that your team members see themselves in it.

BE SUPPORTIVE. One of connected communication's basic tenets is that communications be couched in support. This support will strengthen others by fostering an environment that encourages risk taking, collaboration, self-leadership, and recognition.

ENGAGE A TEAM. Connected communication binds humans together. It is immensely powerful in recruiting, engaging, and inspiring team members to realize your organizational vision.

CREATE ACCOUNTABILITY. Connected communication greatly enables organizational culture and systems that require each individual to contribute his or her share within a collaborative environment. It eliminates the biggest excuse hindering accountability: "I didn't know."

Connected communication also enhances your ability to:

BE CREDIBLE. Connected communication, steeped in "what is," facilitates the building of trust. Team members see the consistency and congruency in your words and behavior, and develop a deep confidence in your abilities and character.

BE PEOPLE-ORIENTED. Connected communication, with its grounding in empathy, can only be accomplished with an open heart and genuine love for people.

BE ENERGETIC. The deeper connection you form with your team members through connected communication fuels you with a deeper sense of purpose and energy to accomplish your vision.

BE CURIOUS. The practice of empathy, which is all about learning at a deep level, inspires you to seek an understanding of everything and everyone in your life.

BE COURAGEOUS. As a connected communicator, an expert at understanding others at a deep level and communicating with them in a purposeful, honest, and supportive way, you will find yourself excelling at the tough communications and thus you will be better able to make the tough calls and perform the tough tasks.

BUILD A VALUES-BASED CORE. Communicating only in a connected manner allows you to effectively convey to your team members, and instill within them, a strong sense of your organization's "stake in the ground" (Collins and Porras 1994, 54).

BUILD A PLAN. Having created and defined the optimal path connecting your vision to results, you will now be able to convey that plan to your team in a clear and inspiring way.

BUILD A RESPONSIVE STRUCTURE. Connected communication is critical to building both the permeability and flexibility necessary in your organization for surviving in our high velocity, highly complex, interconnected existence. The connected communicator always has open ears, eyes, and a mind for identifying conditions outside of him or her.

PRODUCE RESULTS. Connected communication, with its grounding in presence, clarity, and honesty, is a powerful aid to achieving your vision in the most efficient, holistic manner.

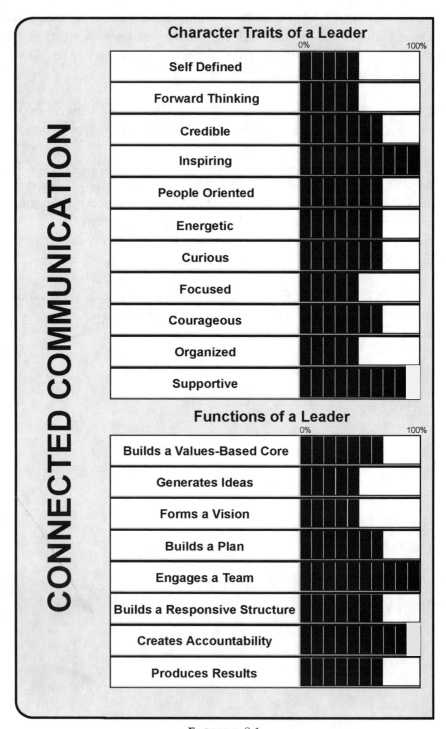

FIGURE 8.1

CHAPTER 9

BECOMING A HIGH-IMPACT LEADER

The Eight Drivers of the

High-Impact Leader

Much of what I do as an executive coach, strategic advisor, and entrepreneur involves determining where my client or company is today, where my client or company wants to be, and the optimal path connecting the two points.

In terms of leadership, I have assumed throughout this book that high-impact leadership is where you, as leaders and aspiring leaders, want to be. We can quibble about the precise character traits and functions that should be ascribed to the high-impact leader, but I believe from my experience with all the major leadership approaches and scores of others, as well as from working with thousands of leaders of all levels of effectiveness, that they all distill down to something resembling the traits and functions I have discussed in this book. They are graphically represented in figure 9.1.

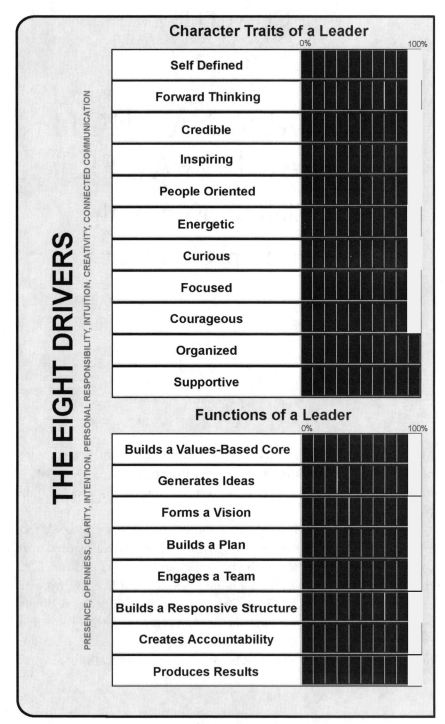

FIGURE 9.1

WHERE ARE YOU TODAY?

The next question, then, is "Where are you today?" By definition, leadership involves an effect upon others. The most accurate description of where you are now as a leader must come from them.

THE SOURCE OF LEADERSHIP ASSESSMENT SURVEY

The Source of Leadership Assessment™ is a powerful tool for determining how well you embody the traits and perform the functions of a high-impact leader. It includes a 360-degree survey of five to ten key leadership constituents, calculator, and dashboard, and is available for downloading at www.thesourceofleadership.com/downloads.

Depending on your leadership position and circumstances, your survey constituents might include your direct reports, the people to whom you report, other team members, board members, investors, volunteers, and key customers and vendors. If you are an aspiring leader, you probably lack direct reports and other subordinate team members, but that shouldn't preclude you from using the assessment. Simply ask constituents to answer the survey as if it were asking about your potential, as opposed to your performance, in the key leadership areas.

Personally introduce the survey to your constituents as an attempt to gather meaningful input on your performance as a leader so that you can improve your leadership, improve the experience of all team members, and enhance the organization. To ensure the most candid feedback— the best picture of "what is"—complete confidence and anonymity should be pledged to the constituents. The survey itself, then, should be administered—distributed, collected, scored, and input—by your assistant or a human resources professional who can be trusted to maintain the confidentiality of the process. That person should destroy the survey responses once they are input, and you should never see or learn of the individual responses.

Constituents should be asked to answer the following questions about you on a scale of 1 to 5, with 1 being the least applicable, or closest to no, and 5 being the most applicable, or closest to yes.

197

1. Does he/she know his/her values? _____

2. Does he/she know his/her beliefs? _____

3. Does he/she have a vision of the future? _____

4. Does he/she express these values, beliefs, and vision clearly? _____

5. Is he/she self-defined? _____

6. Does he/she envision exciting, positive possibilities for the future? _____

7. Is he/she forward thinking? _____

8. Is he/she competent? _____

9. Does he/she display consistency and congruency in his/her words and behavior, such that others have a deep confidence in his/her abilities and character? _____

10. Does he/she have credibility? _____

11. Does he/she listen deeply to others to discover a common purpose among team members and the organization? _____

12. Does he/she give life to his/her organizational vision by communicating it so that his/her team members see themselves in it? _____

13. Is he/she inspiring? _____

14. Is he/she openhearted, with a genuine love for people? _____

15. Is he/she people oriented? _____

16. Does he/she have a deep reservoir of positive energy at all times? _____

17. Is he/she energetic? _____

18. Is he/she inquisitive and eager to learn? _____

19. Is he/she curious? _____

20. Is he/she able to concentrate his/her energy and attention in the pursuit of an objective? _____

21. Is he/she focused? _____

22. Is he/she able to make the tough calls and perform the tough tasks? _____

23. Does he/she have an appetite for taking risks? _____

24. Is he/she courageous? _____

25. Is he/she able to coordinate and direct activities in a functional, structured whole? _____

26. Is he/she organized? _____

27. Does he/she strengthen others by fostering an environment that encourages risk taking, collaboration, self-leadership, and recognition? _____

28. Does he/she facilitate team members in transforming challenges into personal growth? _____

29. Is he/she supportive? _____

30. Do his/her team members have a clear sense of the organization's purpose? _____

31. Do his/her team members have a clear sense of the organization's values? _____

32. Has he/she built a values-based core in the organization? _____

33. Is he/she a thought leader, identifying new associations and connections, and originating new or alternative concepts, approaches, processes, and objectives? _____

34. Is he/she a generator of ideas? _____

35. Does he/she process ideas and possibilities into an organizational objective? _____

36. Does he/she form the vision for the organization? _____

37. Does he/she create and define the optimal path connecting his/her vision to results? _____

38. Does he/she build a plan for achieving the organization's results? _____

39. Does he/she recruit team members successfully? _____

40. Does he/she inspire team members to realize his/her vision? _____

41. Does he/she engage team members successfully? _____

42. Has he/she created a permeable, flexible, and responsive structure that is highly adaptive to changing conditions? _____

43. Has he/she fostered a culture and implemented systems requiring each individual to contribute his or her share within a collaborative environment? _____

44. Has he/she created accountability in the organization? _____

45. Has he/she achieved his/her vision in the most efficient, holistic, and measurable manner? _____

46. Has he/she produced results? _____

THE SOURCE OF LEADERSHIP ASSESSMENT CALCULATOR AND DASHBOARD

Scores for each of the questions are then entered into The Source of Leadership Assessment calculator, which generates your scores for each character trait and function of high-impact leadership. This, in turn, will generate The Source of Leadership Assessment dashboard that will display how well, in the opinion of your closest leadership constituents, you embody the character traits and perform the functions of a high-impact leader.

THE OPTIMAL PATH TO HIGH-IMPACT LEADERSHIP

This section will help you identify the driver or drivers in which you are strong or which need strengthening so that you can become a high-impact leader. Your scores will clearly identify the character traits that you embody or lack, as well as the functions you perform well or which you need to improve. References to specific chapters guide you to drivers you need to develop. You will note that referrals are not made to chapter 1, the driver of presence. Because presence provides the foundation for all other drivers—openness, clarity, intention, personal responsibility, intuition, creativity, and connected communication—you should work to develop presence whenever any other drivers need attention.

QUESTIONS 1–5. If scores for questions 1 through 5 average less than 4, or 80 percent, this is evidence you may be less self-defined than one normally expects of a high-impact leader. You might consider paying attention to the drivers of clarity (chapter 3) and intuition (chapter 6), and possibly to your levels of intention (chapter 4) and personal responsibility (chapter 5).

QUESTIONS 6–7. If scores for questions 6 and 7 average less than 4, or 80 percent, this indicates you may be less forward thinking than the typical high-impact leader. You might look more closely at the driver of openness (chapter 2), and possibly at your levels of clarity (chapter 3), intention (chapter 4), personal responsibility (chapter 5), intuition (chapter 6), and creativity (chapter 7).

QUESTIONS 8–10. If scores for questions 8 through 10 average less than 4, or 80 percent, this suggests you may be less credible than you would like as a high-impact leader. You may want to look closely at the driver of personal responsibility (chapter 5), and possibly at your levels of openness (chapter 2), clarity (chapter 3), intention (chapter 4), intuition (chapter 6), creativity (chapter 7), and connected communication (chapter 8).

QUESTIONS 11–13. If scores for questions 11 through 13 average less than 4, or 80 percent, this is evidence you may be less inspiring than would be expected of a high-impact leader. You might consider paying attention to the drivers of intuition (chapter 6), creativity (chapter 7), and connected communication (chapter 8). You might also look at your levels of openness (chapter 2), clarity (chapter 3), intention (chapter 4), and personal responsibility (chapter 5).

QUESTIONS 14–15. If scores for questions 14 and 15 average less than 4, or 80 percent, this indicates you may be less people oriented than a high-impact leader normally is. You might look closely at the driver of clarity (chapter 3), and possibly at your levels of openness (chapter 2), intention (chapter 4), personal responsibility (chapter 5), intuition (chapter 6), and connected communication (chapter 8).

QUESTIONS 16–17. If scores for questions 16 and 17 average less than 4, or 80 percent, this suggests you may be less energetic than the typical high-impact leader. You may find the solution in the driver of creativity (chapter 7), and possibly in the drivers of openness (chapter 2), clarity (chapter 3), intention (chapter 4), intuition (chapter 6), and connected communication (chapter 8).

QUESTIONS 18–19. If scores for questions 18 and 19 average less than 4, or 80 percent, this is evidence you may be less curious than you need to be as a high-impact leader. You might consider focusing on the driver of openness (chapter 2), and possibly on your levels of clarity (chapter 3), intuition (chapter 6), creativity (chapter 7), and connected communication (chapter 8).

QUESTIONS 20–21. If scores for questions 20 and 21 average less than 4, or 80 percent, you may be less focused than the typical high-impact leader. You might consider paying attention to the driver of intention (chapter 4), and possibly to your level of clarity (chapter 3).

QUESTIONS 22–24. If scores for questions 22 through 24 average less than 4, or 80 percent, this suggests you may be showing less courage than normally seen in a high-impact leader. You might look at the driver of personal responsibility (chapter 5), and possibly at your levels of clarity (chapter 3), intuition (chapter 6), creativity (chapter 7), and connected communication (chapter 8).

QUESTIONS 25–26. If scores for questions 25 and 26 average less than 4, or 80 percent, you may not be as organized as the typical high-impact leader. You might focus on the driver of intention (chapter 4), and possibly on your levels of clarity (chapter 3) and creativity (chapter 7).

QUESTIONS 27–29. If scores for questions 27 through 29 average less than 4, or 80 percent, this is evidence you may be less supportive than one typically expects of a high-impact leader. You might find your solution in the driver of connected communication (chapter 8), and possibly in your levels of clarity (chapter 3), personal responsibility (chapter 5), and intuition (chapter 6).

QUESTIONS 30–32. If scores for questions 30 through 32 average less than 4, or 80 percent, this is evidence you may be lacking in building the values-based core normally built by a high-impact leader. You might consider looking at the driver of clarity (chapter 3), and possibly at your levels of personal responsibility (chapter 5) and connected communication (chapter 8).

QUESTIONS 33–34. If scores for questions 33 and 34 average less than 4, or 80 percent, you may not be the generator of ideas that typifies the high-impact leader. You might focus on the drivers of openness (chapter 2) and creativity (chapter 7), and possibly on your levels of clarity (chapter 3) and intuition (chapter 6).

QUESTIONS 35–36. If scores for questions 35 and 36 average less than 4, or 80 percent, this suggests you might be weaker in forming an organizational vision than the typical high-impact leader. You might consider paying attention to the drivers of openness (chapter 2), intuition (chapter 6), and creativity (chapter 7), and possibly to your levels of clarity (chapter 3) and personal responsibility (chapter 5).

QUESTIONS 37–38. If scores for questions 37 and 38 average less than 4, or 80 percent, you may not be as strong in building a plan as the normal high-impact leader is. You might focus on the drivers of intention (chapter 4) and personal responsibility (chapter 5), and possibly on your levels of intuition (chapter 6), creativity (chapter 7), and connected communication (chapter 8).

QUESTIONS 39–41. If scores for questions 39 through 41 average less than 4, or 80 percent, this suggests you may be less effective at engaging a team than the typical high-impact leader. You might look at the drivers of clarity (chapter 3) and connected communication (chapter 8), and possibly at your levels of openness (chapter 2), intention (chapter 4), personal responsibility (chapter 5), intuition (chapter 6), and creativity (chapter 7).

QUESTION 42. If scores for question 42 average less than 4, or 80 percent, this indicates you may be less adept at building a responsive organizational structure than a high-impact leader normally is. You might examine the driver of intuition (chapter 6), and possibly your levels of openness (chapter 2), intention (chapter 4), creativity (chapter 7), and connected communication (chapter 8).

QUESTIONS 43–44. If scores for questions 43 and 44 average less than 4, or 80 percent, you may be less effective in creating accountability than is normally expected of a high-impact leader. You might explore the drivers of personal responsibility (chapter 5) and connected communication (chapter 8), and possibly your levels of clarity (chapter 3) and intention (chapter 4).

QUESTIONS 45–46. Finally, if scores for questions 45 and 46 average less than 4, or 80 percent, this suggests you may be producing fewer results than you would like as a high-impact leader. You may want to look closely at the driver of intention (chapter 4), and possibly at your levels of personal responsibility (chapter 5), creativity (chapter 7), and connected communication (chapter 8).

HIGH-IMPACT LEADERSHIP

In the introduction, I suggested a new definition of *leadership* that integrates the self and its energies with external results:

> *Leadership is the process of transforming deep personal energies—internal drivers—into extraordinary interpersonal results. The person who recognizes, accesses, and develops those drivers will first be wholly empowered and fulfilled on the personal level and then, and only then, profoundly effective as a leader of people in today's high velocity, highly complex, and interconnected world.*

In *The Source of Leadership*, you learn how to leverage the eight transformational energies—the personal drivers of presence, openness, clarity, intention, personal responsibility, intuition, creativity, and connected communication—into high-impact leadership. Fueled by the eight drivers of the high-impact leader, you will be more fulfilled and content on a personal level than ever before. You will be extraordinarily effective in your leadership role. Whether you are leading a business, a project, your family, a nonprofit organization, a sports team, political constituents, a military unit, an academic institution, a class of students, or a religious organization, you will find yourself having a greater positive impact than you ever imagined possible. If you aspire to a leadership role, you will find yourself thoroughly prepared for one of the most rewarding experiences of your life because:

YOU WILL BE EXTRAORDINARILY SELF-DEFINED. Your clarity, which has freed you of fear-driven thoughts, emotions, and behaviors, and your acute intuition enable you to know exactly who you are, what you value and believe, your higher purpose, and where you are going. You express yourself, your values and beliefs, your purpose and direction clearly, earning the highest respect of your team members.

YOU WILL BE FORWARD THINKING. Your openness—your willingness to consider every element of "what is" without fear and resistance—

makes you seek out and embrace the unknown future and its possibilities. You envision bolder, more exciting possibilities for you, your team members, and your organization.

YOU WILL BE HIGHLY CREDIBLE. Your personal responsibility empowers—indeed compels—you to speak and act with complete consistency, honesty, and congruency. "Walking the walk" will earn you the respect and dedication of your team members.

YOU WILL INSPIRE YOUR TEAM MEMBERS TO ACHIEVE PREVIOUSLY UNIMAGINABLE HEIGHTS. The combination of your intuition, creativity, and the deep empathy and clear expression of connected communication allows you to see the common purpose binding you, your team members, and your organization, and then to give life to your vision so that your team members see themselves as a vibrant part of it.

YOU WILL BE PEOPLE-ORIENTED. Clarity of thought, emotion, and behavior enables you to understand and love all aspects of yourself, whether in your persona or shadow, which in turn opens your heart to others.

YOU WILL BE ENERGETIC. Creativity, by definition one of the fundamental energies of life, restores, regenerates, and invigorates you. You'll have a deep reservoir of positive energy and the ability to generate new energy whenever necessary.

YOU WILL BE INTENSELY CURIOUS. Unbounded by fears that close the mind, you will constantly seek out the new and unknown.

YOU WILL BE HIGHLY FOCUSED. Your practice of intention will concentrate your energy and attention in the pursuit of your personal and organizational objectives.

YOU WILL BE COURAGEOUS. Driven by personal responsibility—complete ownership of "what is"—you will find it easy to make the tough calls, perform the tough tasks, and take risks.

YOU WILL BE ORGANIZED. Practiced intention, with the heightened awareness and energetic force it brings to you, enables you to coordinate and direct activities necessary to achieve your objectives in a functional, structured whole.

YOU WILL BE SUPPORTIVE. Connected communication, grounded in empathy and support for others, fosters an environment of risk taking, collaboration, self-leadership, and recognition that strengthens your team members.

YOU WILL BUILD A VALUES-BASED CORE. With the security that clarity of thought, emotion, and behavior brings—that there is only one master in your life whom you must please—you are able to translate your own self-definition into your organization's and team members' ability to define precisely, in the words of James C. Collins and Jerry Porras, "who we are … what we stand for … what we are all about" (Collins and Porras 1994, 54).

YOU WILL GENERATE MYRIAD IDEAS. Fueled by openness and creativity, you will be a thought leader, identifying new connections, and originating new ways of thinking and behaving.

YOU WILL FORM A VISION. Your fearless openness and flourishing creativity, as well as your highly developed intuition that allows you to see beyond what the rational mind illuminates, drive your ability to process ideas and possibilities into highly valuable organizational objectives.

YOU WILL BUILD A PLAN. Practiced intention, combined with personal responsibility and its resulting feeling of control and belief that you can have an effect, drives your ability to create and define for your team members the optimal path connecting your vision to results.

YOU WILL ENGAGE A TEAM. Clarity of thought, emotion, and behavior, achieved through thorough knowledge of yourself—your persona and shadow—combined with the connected communication that binds humans together, empowers you to engage the hearts of your team members. Their minds and bodies follow closely.

YOU WILL BUILD A RESPONSIVE STRUCTURE. The powerful insight of intuition drives your ability to build a structure ideally suited for the dynamic, high velocity, highly complex world in which we live. This permeable structure is highly adaptive and responsive to rapidly changing conditions.

YOU WILL CREATE A HIGH DEGREE OF ACCOUNTABILITY. Your unwavering personal responsibility inspires your team members to take responsibility and supports a culture and systems that require each individual to contribute his or her share within a collaborative environment. Connected communication eliminates the biggest excuse hindering accountability: "I didn't know."

YOU WILL PRODUCE RESULTS. A disciplined practice of intention, combined with all of the traits and functions discussed above, translates into a highly positive impact.

YOU WILL BE A HIGH-IMPACT LEADER. You will have leveraged the eight personal drivers deep within you into positive change in your personal life, your organization, the lives of your team members, and ultimately in the lives of all other people in this interconnected world in which we live. May the speed of light, the support of the universe, and endless energy be with you.

Join like-minded leaders and aspiring leaders at www .thesourceofleadership.com for a premier leadership blog, downloads, a recommended reading list, and notification of The Source of Leadership *programs, news, and events.*

REFERENCES

Alexander, C., P. Robinson, and M. Rainforth. 1994. Treating and preventing alcohol, nicotine, and drug abuse through Transcendental Meditation: A review and statistical meta-analysis. *Alcoholism Treatment Quarterly* 11:13–87.

Bach, R. 1977. *Illusions*. New York: Dell.

Bates v. State Bar of Arizona, 433 U.S. 350 (1977).

Benson, H., and R. K. Wallace. 1970. Decreased drug abuse with Transcendental Meditation. Paper presented to the International Symposium on Drug Abuse for Physicians, University of Michigan, August 1970, and to the House Select Committee on Crime, printed in *Hearings Before the Select Committee on Crime of the House of Representatives*, Ninety-second Congress, first session, 1971.

Berrettini, R. 1976. The effects of the Transcendental Meditation program on short-term recall performance. Master's thesis, Wilkes College.

Bleick, C., and A. Abrams. 1987. The Transcendental Meditation program and criminal recidivism in California. *Journal of Criminal Justice* 15:211–30.

Bly, R. 1988. *A Little Book on the Human Shadow*. San Francisco: HarperSanFrancisco.

Burnham, S. 2002. *The Path of Prayer*. New York: Viking Compass.

Cameron, J. 1992. *The Artist's Way: A Spiritual Path to Higher Creativity*. New York: Tarcher/Penguin Putnam.

Chouinard, Y. 2005. *Let My People Go Surfing*. New York: Penguin.

Ciaramicoli, A., and K. Ketcham. 2001. *The Power of Empathy*. New York: Plume/Penguin Putnam.

Collins, J. 2001. *Good to Great*. New York: HarperCollins.

Collins, J. C., and J. I. Porras. 1994. *Built to Last*. New York: Harper Business.

Conlin, M. 2004. I'm a bad boss? Blame my dad. *Business Week*, May 10, 60–61.

Cooper, M., and M. Aygen. 1979. Transcendental Meditation in the management of hypercholesterolemia. *Journal of Human Stress* 5(4):24–27.

Cranson, R., D. Orme-Johnson, J. Gackenbach, M. Dillbeck, C. Jones, and C. Alexander. 1991. Transcendental Meditation and improved performance on intelligence-related measures: A longitudinal study. *Personality and Individual Differences* 12(10):1105–16.

Day, L. 1997. *Practical Intuition*. New York: Broadway Books/Bantam Doubleday Dell.

Der Hovanesian, M. 2003. Zen and the art of corporate productivity. *Business Week*, July 28, 56.

Dunne, B. J. 1991. Co-operator experiments with an REG device. (Technical note PEAR 91005.) Princeton Engineering Anomalies Research, Princeton University, School of Engineering/Applied Science.

Dunne, B., and R. Jahn. 1992. Experiments in remote human/machine interaction. *Journal of Scientific Exploration* 6:311–32.

Emoto, M. 2005. *The True Power of Water*. Hillsboro, OR: Beyond Words Publishing.

Engel, B. 2005. *Breaking the Cycle of Emotional Abuse*. Hoboken, NJ: Wiley.

Frew, D. 1974. Transcendental Meditation and productivity. *Academy of Management Journal* 17:362–68.

Gettleman, J. 2006. Annan of UN blames "lack of leadership" for global warming. *International Herald Tribune*, November 16, sec. NE, ed. 3, 8.

Goldsmith, M. 2004. Leave it at the stream. *Fast Company*. May 103.

Gordon, T. 2001. *Leadership Effectiveness Training*. 2nd ed. New York: Perigee/Penguin Putnam.

Greenleaf, R. 1977. *Servant Leadership*. Mahwah, NJ: Paulist Press.

Hawkins, D. 1995. *Power vs. Force*. Carlsbad, CA: Hay House.

Hill, N. 1960. *Think and Grow Rich*. New York: Fawcett/Random House.

Jaworski, J. 1996. *Synchronicity*. San Francisco: Berrett-Koehler.

Jung, C. 1959. *The Archetypes and the Collective Unconscious*. New York: Pantheon Books.

Kouzes, J., and B. Posner. 2002. *The Leadership Challenge*. 3rd ed. San Francisco: Jossey-Bass.

Lashinsky, A. 2007. Search and enjoy. *Fortune*, January 22, 70–82.

McGuire, W. J. 1969. Attitude and attitude change. In *Handbook of Social Psychology*, ed. Gardner Lindsey and Elliot Aronson. 2nd ed. (3 vols.) 3:136–314. Reading, MA: Addison-Wesley.

Miller, W. A. 1989. *Your Golden Shadow*. San Francisco: Harper & Row.

Mills, W., and J. Farrow. 1981. The Transcendental Meditation technique and acute experimental pain. *Psychosomatic Medicine* 43(2):157–64.

Montana, J., and T. Mitchell. 2005. *The Winning Spirit*. New York: Random House.

Muehlman, J., S. Nidich, B. Reilly, and C. Cole. 1988. Relationship of the practice of the Transcendental Meditation technique to academic achievement. Paper presented at the annual meeting of the Mid-Western Educational Research Association, Chicago, IL.

Olson, W. 1991. Better living through litigation. *The Public Interest*, Spring: 76–87.

Orme-Johnson, D. 1987. Medical care utilization and the Transcendental Meditation program. *Psychosomatic Medicine* 49(1):493–507.

Palmer, P. 1990. Leading from within: Reflections on spirituality and leadership. Transcription of address delivered at the Annual Celebration Dinner of the Indiana Office for Campus Ministries, March.

Schneider, R., C. Alexander, and R. Wallace. 1992. In search of an optimal behavioral treatment for hypertension: A review and focus on Transcendental Meditation. In *Personality, Elevated Blood Pressure, and Essential Hypertension*, ed. S. Johnson, W. Gentry, and S. Julius, 291–316. Washington, DC: Hemisphere Publishing.

Sellers, P. 2006. MySpace cowboys. *Fortune*, September 4, 66–74.

Senge, P. 1990. *The Fifth Discipline*. New York: Currency Doubleday.

Simon, D., S. Oparil, and C. Kimball. 1974. The Transcendental Meditation program and essential hypertension. Hypertension Clinic and Department of Psychiatry, Pritzker School of Medicine, University of Chicago, Chicago, IL.

Thich Nhat Hanh. 2001. *Essential Writings*. Maryknoll, NY: Orbis Books.

Tichy, N., with E. Cohen. 1997. *The Leadership Engine*. New York: HarperBusiness Essentials.

Travis, F. 1979. Creative thinking and the Transcendental Meditation technique. *Journal of Creative Behavior* 13(3):169–80.

Wallace, R. 1970. The physiological effects of Transcendental Meditation: A proposed fourth major state of consciousness. Ph.D. diss. University of California at Los Angeles, Department of Physiology, n. 1, p. 54.

Wallace, R., and H. Benson. 1972. The physiology of meditation. *Scientific American*, February, 84–90.

Wallace, R., M. Dillbeck, E. Jacobe, and B. Harrington. 1982. The effects of the Transcendental Meditation and TM-Sidhi program on the aging process. *International Journal of Neuroscience* 16:53–58.

Washington, J., ed. 1986. *A Testament of Hope: The Essential Writings and Speeches of Martin Luther King Jr.* New York: HarperCollins.

Wheatley, M. J. 1999. *Leadership and the New Science.* San Francisco: Berrett-Koehler.

Zukav, G. 1979. *The Dancing Wu Li Masters.* New York: William Morrow.

Zweig, C., and J. Abrams. 1991. *Meeting the Shadow.* New York: Tarcher/Putnam.

David M. Traversi is the founder and managing director of 2020 Growth Partners, LLC (www.2020gp.com), which offers executive coaching, strategic advisory, merchant banking, and leadership development services to executives and companies across the United States. He has worked as a chief executive of operating companies, a trial lawyer, a commercial lender, an investment banker, private company investor. In addition, he has started several successful companies in diverse industries. Traversi holds an MBA from the Haas School of Business at the University of California, Berkeley, and a JD from the King Hall School of Law at the University of California, Davis.